# EGYPT

## YESTERDAY AND TODAY

LITHOGRAPHS BY DAVID ROBERTS, R.A.

THE AMERICAN UNIVERSITY IN CAIRO PRESS

David Roberts R.A.    L' Hagÿe Cairo.

Grand Portico of the Temple of Philæ — Nubia

Interior of the Temple of Abou Simbel
Novr 9th 1836 — Nubia.

View from under the Portico of Temple of Edfou, Upper Egypt.

David Roberts. R.A.

L. Haghe. lith.

*David Roberts R.A. [London]*

*Portico of the Temple Edfou Upper Egypt. Nov 25 1838*

2-3  *The interior
of the temple of Isis.*

4-5  *The interior
of the great temple of
Abu Simbel.*

6-7 *The pylon
of the temple of Edfu,
from the pronaos.*

8-9  *The pronaos
of the temple of Edfu.*

# EGYPT
## *YESTERDAY AND TODAY*

### LITHOGRAPHS BY DAVID ROBERTS, R.A.

**Text by**
Fabio Bourbon

**Photographs by**
Antonio Attini

**Graphic design by**
Anna Galliani

**Translation by**
A.B.A., Milano

## CONTENTS

**Thanks are due to the following people
for their valuable contributions to this book:
Nabil Osman, President of Egypt's General Board
of Information; Gamal Shafik from Cairo Press
Center; Ahmed Aly Abod El Gheit, Ambassador
of Egypt in Rome; Ali Hashem,
Press Counsellor at the Egyptian Embassy in
Rome and Bernard Shapero.**

First published in Egypt in 1996 by
The American University in Cairo Press
113 Kasr el Aini Street
Cairo, Egypt

© 1996 White Star S.r.l.

This edition published by arrangement with
White Star S.r.l.
Vercelli, Italy

Dar el Kutub No 8266/96
ISBN 977 424 408 7

Printed in Italy

# INTRODUCTION

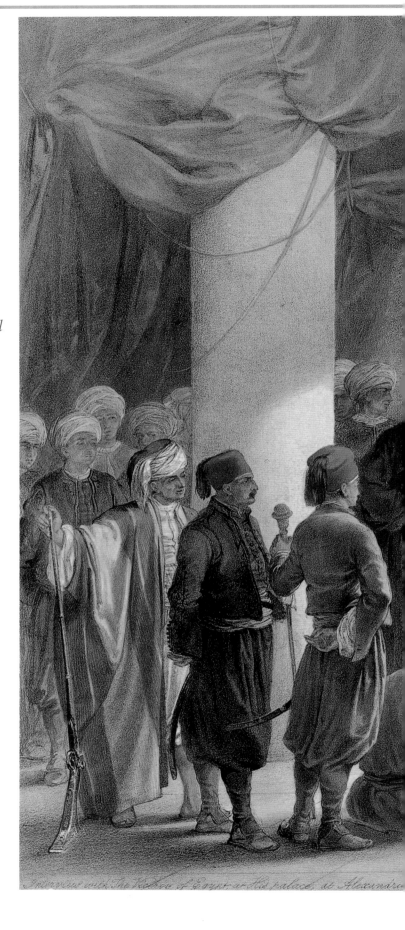

*T**his book is the natural sequel to* The Holy Land Yesterday and Today, *the first edition of that was published in 1994; this volume contains 124 lithographs that, together with the 123 published in the previous volume, constitute the full reproduction of the six volumes of lithographs taken from the original drawings by David Roberts, which were published by Francis Graham Moon in London between 1842 and 1849.*

*Once again, each lithograph is accompanied by a photo taken by brilliant young photographer Antonio Attini who, more than a century and a half after the Scottish artist's expedition, has endeavored to recreate the original views in a kind of imaginary journey between past and present. The only exceptions are the monuments that have been destroyed or removed from their original sites and some situations that, for historical reasons, can no longer be reproduced.*

*As we wrote in the introduction to the previous volume, David Roberts was unfairly forgotten soon after his death, like many other British artists of the Victorian era, and only rediscovered recently by art critics. However, collectors' interest in his work has never flagged, and his pictures fetch very high prices. Unanimously described as one of the masters of the 19th-century British romantic school, Roberts is now known to the general public for*
*the epic grandeur and incredible detail of all his views. Despite his extensive artistic production, Roberts's fame is still mainly due to the lithographs based on the drawings he made during his long pilgrimage to Egypt and the Holy Land. Though unjustifiably limited, this fame is not undeserved, as this monumental work constitutes a masterpiece that is still of great interest. Although many other Westerners had visited the archaeological remains of Egypt before him, Roberts was the first whose priority was systematic exploration of the major Egyptian and Islamic monumental sites in the country, with a view to publishing a popular work. No one had ever drawn temples, necropolises, mosques and minarets with such scrupulous care, reproducing every detail with a precision that today would be called photographic. It is therefore ironic that his art was at least partly overshadowed by a sensational invention dating from the very year when Roberts commenced his journey to Egypt and the Holy Land; in fact, it was in 1838 that Frenchman Louis-Jacques Daguerre successfully made the first photographic plate. The lithographs reproduced here, made with extraordinary skill by Louis Haghe with the aid of his brother and a few other assistants, appeared in the hand-painted deluxe edition, supplied*

After a long search and some hard bargaining, Roberts's ambitious project eventually found the right publisher in Francis Graham Moon. In order to finance the printing of the monumental work, Moon recruited private subscribers who would receive the large, hand-colored deluxe edition of the lithographs. Between 1842 and 1849, on the basis of sketches made on the spot and aided by his excellent memory, Roberts produced drawings that Louis Haghe gradually turned into prints published monthly. The complete work consisted of six folio volumes, comprising 247 lithographs, including six frontispieces. The first three volumes, dedicated to Queen Victoria and entitled The Holy Land, Syria, Idumea, Egypt and Nubia, *mainly contained the subjects Roberts had drawn during the second half of his journey, from the Sinai peninsula to Beirut; the original text was written by Rev. George Croly. The other three volumes, dedicated to King Louis Philippe of France, appeared under the title* Egypt and Nubia, From Drawings Made on the Spot by David Roberts, R.A. *The lithographs portrayed the monumental sites of pharaonic Egypt and the mosques of Cairo, and the text was written by William Brockedon. The lithograph shown here depicts Roberts's meeting with the pasha of Egypt on May 16, 1839, when he stopped over in Alexandria on his return from Beirut. Logically, this illustration should have concluded the previous volume,* The Holy Land Yesterday and Today; *however, in view of its geographical location and incompatibility of form with the rest of the works, we considered that it was more logical to include it as a separate plate in this volume. The informal meeting arranged by the British consul in Cairo, Colonel Campbell, lasted about 20 minutes, and left an indelible impression on the artist. Roberts did not have pencil and paper with him, and had to reconstruct the scene from memory. The pasha, on the left, is sitting cross-legged, while the senior members of his entourage stand behind him; the men sitting on the sofa on the right are Colonel Campbell, Lieutenant Waghorn, Roberts himself leaning slightly forward, and two English officers.*

on subscription to a number of dignitaries of the period; the number of copies printed is unknown, but it was certainly a very limited edition. The second edition was printed in black, white and ocher, and was followed by numerous reprints in a smaller size.

This volume retains the general layout of its predecessor; we therefore consider that apart from the artistic value of the lithographs reproduced here, its main interest again lies in the fact that they are arranged in the strictest possible chronological sequence, from Roberts's arrival in Alexandria on September 24, 1838 to his departure from Cairo on February 6, 1839.

In an attempt to reconstruct the author's experiences during his journey, we have divided his itinerary into three separate stages, shown in different colors on the map opposite, each of which corresponds to one chapter. In our view this is not an arbitrary division dictated by the wish for classification at all costs or a desire for symmetry with The Holy Land Yesterday and Today, as the journal demonstrates that Roberts planned his long expedition to Egypt in accordance with a detailed schedule that fell into three different stages.

Roberts had neither the time nor the money to be able to afford any delay; he was also fully aware that his artistic success and his future in general depended on the outcome of the venture. From Alexandria, he therefore traveled to Cairo, and from there in the direction of Abu Simbel, without delay; as he sailed up the Nile he only stopped when strictly necessary. Having arrived safe and sound at his long-awaited destination, the fabulous rock temple excavated by order of Rameses II in the heart of Nubia, Roberts embarked on the return journey with a calmer spirit, though he never stopped very long in one place. His long stay in Cairo was entirely devoted to the masterpieces of Islamic architecture, which he had decided to document with the same precision with which he had just portrayed the magnificent ruins of pharaonic Egypt. As a matter of fact, the work he accomplished during those weeks spent in the Egyptian capital before his departure for the Holy Land exceeded even his own expectations. In view of all these factors, we have opened each chapter of this volume with one of the three frontispieces that appeared in the first edition of the work published by Graham Moon, depicting the places that most impressed Roberts – Abu Simbel, Karnak and Cairo – and the three different emotional experiences he underwent there. The original division of the work into three volumes encouraged our attempt at a chronological reinterpretation of Roberts's very unusual artistic and human experience. The method we followed in reconstructing his itinerary was the same as used for the previous volume, basically involving a detailed study of Roberts's travel journals (which have sadly never been published in full, and are now housed in manuscript form at the National Scottish Library in Edinburgh) and a geographical reconnaissance of each location. Our purpose, in the quite frequent cases in which there were gaps in Roberts's written notes, was to establish the feasibility of the schedule and the logic of the sequences we have devised. Especially in the Cairo chapter, we faced considerable problems because the basic information was incomplete and great changes have occurred in the city in the meantime; as a result of earthquakes, collapses and demolition, no trace remains of some buildings, while the appearance of others is greatly altered, sometimes making it impossible to match the lithograph with its exact photographic equivalent. Equally, Roberts published his prints without following any chronological order, and the fact that many of the lithographs are undated (or incorrectly dated as a result of errors by the engraver) presented considerable difficulties in composing the most reliable possible sequence of pictures; however, we trust that our attempt has at least partly succeeded in recreating the fascination of Roberts's remarkable journey.

*Fabio Bourbon*

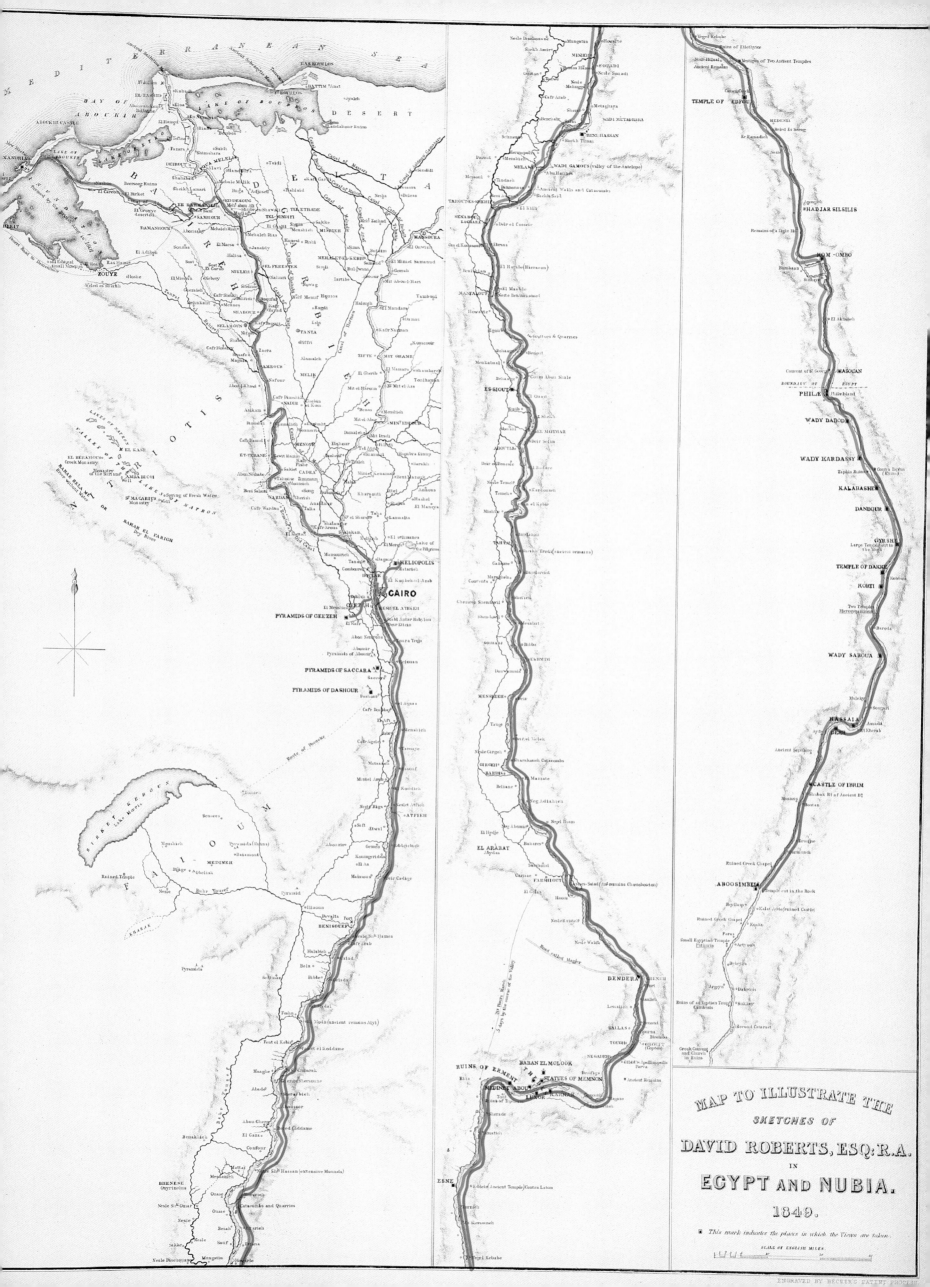

MAP TO ILLUSTRATE THE

SKETCHES OF

DAVID ROBERTS, ESQ: R.A.

IN

EGYPT AND NUBIA.

1849.

* *This mark indicates the places in which the Views are taken.*

SCALE OF ENGLISH MILES.

ENGRAVED BY BECKER'S PATENT PROCESS

# LIST OF PLATES

# THE LIFE OF DAVID ROBERTS

*D*avid Roberts, who was to be described as one of the greatest landscape artists of the 19th century, was born on October 24 1796, in Stockbridge, near Edinburgh.

His natural artistic talent emerged at a very early age, encouraged by his mother, who enjoyed telling her son stories about her native town of St. Andrew, where the ruins of a famous cathedral and a monastery complex stood. When little David, fascinated by some colorful circus posters he had seen, covered the kitchen walls with rows of animals and other figures expertly drawn with red chalk, even his father, a humble cobbler, recognized his remarkable gift. Much to his regret, however, he could not afford to send the boy to school. Roberts was consequently a brilliant self-taught artist; he did not learn all the basic academic skills necessary for an artist's career until he was in his forties. Probably the only person who taught him some of the rudiments of drawing was one Gavin Beugo, a cantankerous, authoritarian decorator recommended to the family by the director of the Edinburgh Trustees Academy, to whom Roberts was apprenticed for seven years. A curious anecdote that confirms his innate artistic gifts dates from that period. Beugo had given his apprentice a pound note to pay a supplier, but when Roberts called on him, he was out. While he waited,

Roberts made a perfect copy of that incredible bill, which he had never been able to observe at close quarters before. Some time later, while his mother was tidying her son's collection of drawings, she found the "forged" note, and, before realizing her mistake, was horrified to think that she had nurtured a thief.

In 1815 Roberts moved to Perth, where he obtained his first real paying job as a professional decorator.

When he returned to Edinburgh the next year, he found a job as assistant set painter in the Pantheon repertory company, with which he traveled all over Scotland. He wrote later that he had fulfilled his greatest aspiration in this way, because as a result of his contact with the amazing world of the theater his imagination took him to distant countries; when he watched performances of Ali Baba and the Forty Thieves, Baghdad seemed to have become familiar to him, with its minarets and the night air smelling sweetly of spices. For the time being, however, he had no reason to believe that he would ever travel to the East.

In 1819 he became official set painter to the Glasgow Theatre Royal, and later held the same position with the Edinburgh Theatre Royal. He married Scottish actress Margaret McLachlan in 1820, but they separated after a very short time together; however, Roberts was

always a good father, devoted to his only daughter Christine, born in 1821, with whom he had a very affectionate relationship. She repaid him when she grew up by rearranging his work and copying out his travel journals. In the last few months of 1821 his fame increased so much that he was engaged by the Drury Lane Theatre in London together with his friend and great rival, Clarkson Stanfield, also destined to become a famous landscape artist. In 1824 Roberts had the satisfaction of seeing his first oil painting, a view of Dryburgh Abbey, exhibited at the British Institution. Two years later, the artist was engaged by Covent Garden opera house. In the meantime, his sets for a performance of Mozart's The Seraglio had met with remarkable international success.

During that period, his View of Rouen Cathedral was presented to the public at the Royal Academy, and his paintings began to be widely praised by the critics; even the Times spoke very well of his work. In the meantime, Roberts had become involved in the foundation of the Society of British Artists, of which he was elected president in 1831. Despite the increasing number of commissions he received from private patrons, during the early part of his career Roberts had many opportunities to travel in Europe, bringing back numerous sketches, drawings

and watercolors that would serve as subjects for his paintings. In addition to his famous views of places and monuments in France, Germany and the Netherlands, he also drew his native Scotland; during his frequent visits to his parents' home he visited all the most glorious Scottish ruins, which inspired some of his best paintings. Among other things, these expeditions led to an excellent series of copperplate etchings, which were sadly never reprinted after the first edition. Delighted by increasing public recognition, he gave up his work as a set designer in 1830, and restricted his field of activity to the far more remunerative studio work. Among other things, during that period he completed a series of drawings commissioned by Sir Bulwer Lytton, entitled Pilgrims of the Rhine.

In 1832, on the advice of his friend David Wilkie, he decided to visit Spain, then a little-known country, which was to prove a generous source of inspiration for his creative urges. During his journey, which lasted nearly two years, Roberts visited nearly all the major Spanish cities, including Madrid, Toledo, Granada, Malaga, Seville and Gibraltar. As he traveled he tirelessly drew ruins and monuments dating from a wide variety of periods, devoting particular attention to Moorish art and the local flamboyant Gothic style.

In 1837 a selection of these

views appeared under the title Picturesque Sketches of Spain; 1,200 copies were sold in only two months, which would have made the artist a small fortune if he had not been defrauded by the publisher. However, the Spanish experience paved the way for him to acquire a sound international reputation, and also brought about his meeting with Louis Haghe, a young engraver of Belgian descent with outstanding talent, although his right arm was crippled, with whom he was to have a long and fruitful partnership in the years to come. During his trip to Spain Roberts traveled as far as Morocco, and the charm of that country awakened his interest in new and wider horizons. He gathered together all his savings, and after obtaining detailed information about local customs and the political and social situation in Egypt, Palestine and Syria, in August 1838 he embarked on the long expedition that was to make him so famous that his name went down in the annals of history. He set off for Paris, then continued along the Rhône Valley to Marseilles, where he arrived on September 11, and embarked on a steamship bound for Civitavecchia in Italy. In his travel journal he

Presented to Mr Henry Bicknell

expressed his regret that he had come so close to Rome without being able to see it.

The ship called at Malta and the Cyclades, and at the end of September he finally disembarked at the port of Alexandria. For three months he sailed up the Nile on a chartered boat, managing to draw all the main archaeological sites in the area, and pressed on as far as Nubia and Abu Simbel. On December 21, Roberts was in Cairo with over a hundred drawings and paintings. He spent six weeks in the Egyptian capital, during which time he was the first Westerner allowed to enter a mosque and draw the interior. In Cairo, Roberts met Hanafee Ismail Effendi, a young Egyptian converted to Christianity, who spoke fluent English. The young man accompanied Roberts during the rest of his adventure.

During the same period Roberts also met two British travelers, John Pell and John Kinnear; in February 1839 he agreed to accompany them to Sinai, after which he would go on to the legendary Petra and Palestine. Roberts parted company from Kinnear at Gaza and went on to Jerusalem, where he arrived at Easter; after visiting the Jordan Valley and the main sights of the area he continued north, calling at the Sea of Galilee and the main towns on the Lebanese coast. At Baalbek he contracted a persistent fever that prevented him from visiting Palmyra and forced him to turn back to Beirut, where he embarked for England on May 13, 1839.

On his return home after eleven months' absence he submitted the results of his labors to numerous publishers and received the right kind of interest from Francis Graham Moon, who offered him three thousand pounds to publish the work and supervise the complex task of engraving the plates. The 247 lithographs that composed the six volumes, published between 1842 and 1849, were produced by Louis Haghe on the basis of Roberts's own drawings and comments. The technique used by the engraver for the first edition was particularly laborious, as each print was made by the two-color process and then colored by hand. Roberts mainly profited in terms of fame and glory, as the agreed fee was nothing by comparison with the mammoth task he had undertaken and the discomfort he had experienced during his journey. Two years after his return home, Roberts finally became a full member of the Royal Academy. In the next two decades the artist visited numerous European countries on various occasions, and these travels inspired paintings and engravings displayed with great success in leading galleries, both in Britain and abroad. His huge clientele included many of the leading personalities of the era, and among his friends were famous poets, writers and artists such as Charles Dickens, William Turner and William Thackeray. During his long career he received many coveted prizes and awards, one of the most prestigious of which was the prize awarded at the Paris International Exposition in 1855. The same year, Roberts became an honorary member of the Amsterdam Royal Academy. In 1859 he visited Italy, and the next year he completed a series of oil paintings with the Thames as their theme. During his last journeys to Belgium and Holland he was accompanied by his daughter, Christine, and Louis Haghe. During that period, nearly all his works were either commissioned or sold as soon as they were completed, which demonstrates his continued fame and flourishing financial circumstances. Basking in the love of his daughter and friends and the praise of the critics, David Roberts died of a heart attack at the age of 68 on November 25, 1864 and was buried in Norwood cemetery.

The numerous drawings, sketches and watercolors from which he had always refused to be parted were auctioned by Christie's the next year, and are now in public and private collections all over the world, while his oil paintings are mainly exhibited in leading English and Scottish museums.

Page 20 (top)
This portrait of David Roberts appeared in the first edition of The Holy Land, Syria, Idumea, Egypt and Nubia.

Page 20 (bottom)
In the years following the publication of the opera, Roberts encountered increasing success with the critics and the public, so much so that numerous private individuals commissioned paintings taken from the lithographs. His most famous clients included Queen Victoria, the countess of Warwick and numerous members of the British aristocracy and upper classes. Before beginning a painting, it was Roberts's custom to submit a pen and ink sketch similar to the one shown here (depicting the Temple of Kom Ombo), accompanied by technical data and the size and price of the painting, for the client's approval. These sketches are quite interesting because they give some idea of what the preparatory drawings sketched on the spot by the author during his travels must have looked like.

Pages 22-23
View of the Temple of Dakke, rebuilt at New Saboua.

Pages 24-25
View of the Temple of Luxor.

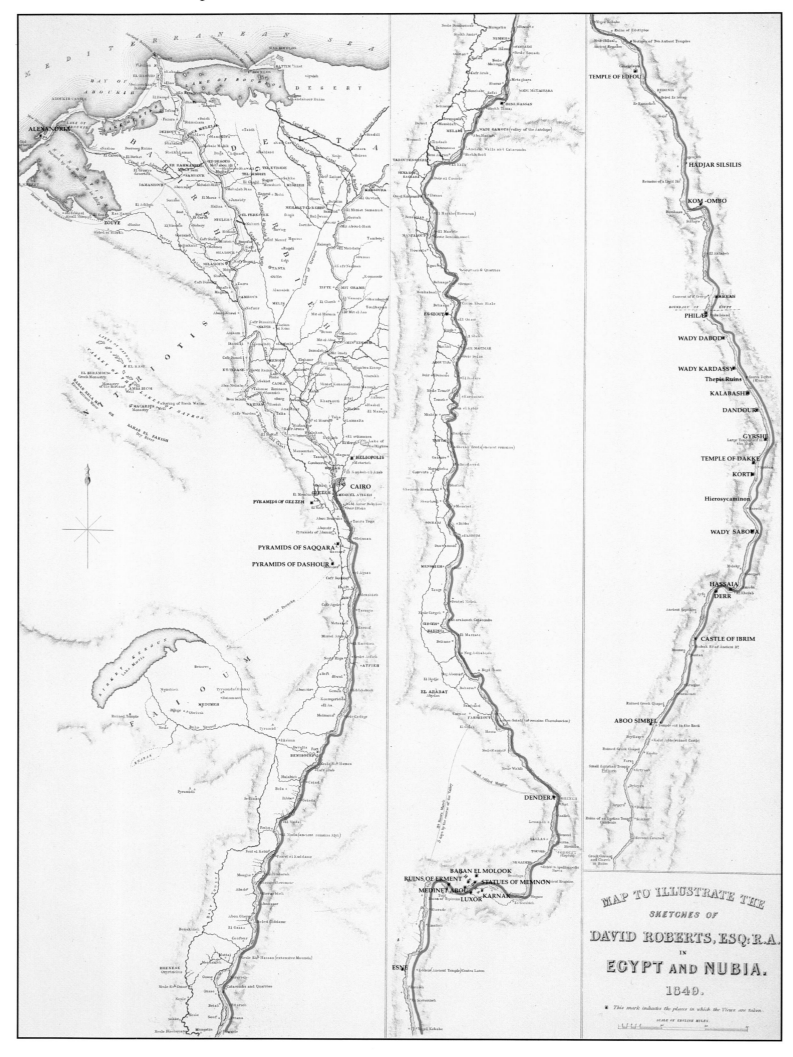

MAP TO ILLUSTRATE THE
SKETCHES OF
DAVID ROBERTS, ESQ: R.A.
IN
EGYPT AND NUBIA.
1849.

FROM DRAWINGS MADE ON THE SPOT BY

## David Roberts, R.A.

WITH HISTORICAL DESCRIPTIONS BY

### WILLIAM BROCKEDON, F.R.S.

LITHOGRAPHED BY

### LOUIS HAGHE.

VOL. 3

Great Gateway, leading to the Temple of Karnac, Thebes.

David Roberts, R.A.

LONDON, F. G. MOON, 20 THREADNEEDLE STREET,
PUBLISHER IN ORDINARY TO HER MAJESTY.
MDCCCXLIX.

# THE PORT OF ALEXANDRIA

Plate 1

*September 24, 1838*

*A*fter spending a great deal of time planning the journey that was to take him away from home for nearly a year, David Roberts left London on August 31, 1838. Following stopovers in France, Italy, Malta and the Cyclades, he eventually reached Alexandria on September 24. The sight of Alexandria left him speechless, it was so different from any other city he had ever seen. He was particularly amazed by the crowds that thronged around the ship and on the wharves: boatmen vociferously offering their services, others transshipping goods and passengers, black porters who would shoulder huge loads for a small reward, and camel drivers who rushed around getting their animals into line amid the most appalling din. On entering the city Roberts saw, mingling together in an indescribable confusion, magnificently dressed Turkish gentlemen, stark naked black slave girls, Greek and Jewish merchants and people of every nationality heading in one direction or another, apparently aimlessly. Though dazed by all this novelty, the Scottish artist remained sufficiently objective to observe that despite the glorious relics of its past, the ancient splendor of Alexandria had long ago declined. The city, with its 600,000 inhabitants, looked more like an anthill than anything else.

**From David Roberts's journal:**

*September 24 - This morning we rose early. Alexandria was right in front of us, with mosques and palm trees that gave it a different atmosphere from any I had ever breathed before... The bay was crowded with a large number of vessels, many of which were warships; our boat was soon surrounded by the most picturesque boatmen I have ever seen...*

# Cleopatra's Needles
# in Alexandria

Plate 2

*September 24–26, 1838*

As soon as he disembarked in Alexandria, Roberts set to work to arrange a voyage up the Nile to Abu Simbel. First of all he chartered a boat that would take him by river to the Delta, from where he intended to travel to Cairo. Preceded by a letter of introduction from the foreign minister that he had obtained at home with the aid of friends in high places, he contacted Colonel Campbell to obtain all possible assistance. Colonel Campbell gave him a very cordial welcome, obtained the documents authorizing him to travel unhindered in Egypt and Nubia, and gave him a great deal of advice that was to prove very useful in the coming months. Egypt, governed by Pasha Mohammed Ali (who had taken power in 1805 after driving out the Turks and had inflicted a resounding defeat even on the English), was an unpredictable country where Western travelers had to cope with every kind of discomfort.

Though absorbed by the numerous preparations for his imminent expedition, Roberts could not suppress his natural artist's curiosity, and on the very day of his arrival he visited the main sights of the great port. This first contact with the monuments of ancient Egypt was not a great success, however, because of their ruined condition, so that only two of them provided suitable subjects for his inspiration: the obelisks of Tuthmosis III and Pompey's Column. Two days later he made some sketches after measuring them accurately; this practice was of great importance in order to reproduce the proportions of the monuments and every structural and decorative element with the greatest precision.

At the time when Roberts visited Alexandria, only one of the two great obelisks, known as Cleopatra's Needles was still standing on its pedestal. This name, though evocative, had no historical foundation but was of popular origin, partly based on the fact that in Arabic these ancient symbols of the generating power of the sun god were generically called messalah (needles).

The two great monoliths were erected by Pharaoh Tuthmosis III in front of the Temple of Amun at Heliopolis, from which they were transferred over fourteen centuries later, by order of Augustus, to decorate the temple erected in Alexandria in honor of Julius Caesar. Of the two obelisks, which stood some 70 feet tall, the one that Roberts saw lying on the ground was taken to London and erected on the Victoria Embankment on September 13, 1878, while the other, donated to the United States in 1869 to mark the opening of the Suez Canal, was erected at Central Park in New York on January 22, 1881.

# POMPEY'S COLUMN AT ALEXANDRIA

Plate 3

*September 24–26, 1838*

On the evening of the 24th, accompanied by a local guide and some Europeans he had just met, Roberts, riding a donkey, reached the ancient citadel of Rhakotis to see the famous Pompey's Column. It did not particularly impress him, but rather suggested neglect and desolation.

The column, which stands 100 feet tall, is erected on an older base made of spoil. The shaft, made of a single piece of red granite, supports a white marble Corinthian capital.

The attribution of this monument to Julius Caesar's great rival Gnaeus Pompeus is based on legend, although it belongs to the right historical period. The column was actually part of the extension to the Serapeum, ordered by Mark Antony to provide new premises for the famous library, which was destroyed in the fire following Caesar's siege of Alexandria.

After numerous trials and tribulations and the permanent ruin of the second library, this surviving element of the great portico was re-erected in AD 296 in honor of the Emperor Diocletian, who had put down a rebellion against the power of Rome. On that occasion a statue may have been placed on the capital.

Generally, according to the notes in his journal, Roberts seems to have been more struck by the local color than the very modest antiquities to be seen in Alexandria. In particular, he was horrified by the sight of the slave market, where lovely Circassians and half-naked black girls were auctioned under the scorching sun.

**From David Roberts's journal:**

*September 24 - Pompey's Column consists of five parts: the pedestal, the plinth, the base, the shaft and the capital. It may originally have been surmounted by a statue; alternatively, it may have been part of the colonnade of a temple, which I think is likely, as it stands on a pile of rubble.*

Pompey's Pillar, Alexandria                                    David Roberts R.A.

# AN ANCIENT WELL
# NEAR NIKLEH

Plate 4

*September 27-29, 1838*

*I*n Alexandria, as well as Colonel Campbell, Roberts met the consul, Robert Thorburn, well known to British travelers of the period because of his unrivaled helpfulness. With their assistance, the Scottish artist was introduced to French explorer and geographer Louis-Maurice-Adolphe Linant de Bellefonds, who accompanied him in his excursions around town, and some Britons, two of whom decided to join his expedition. In Roberts's journal, one of them (a Mr. Vanderhorst) is always referred to as Mr. V; he was a clumsy, chubby gentleman accompanied by a Maltese servant and an Italian chef, who said he was traveling for the sake of his delicate health. Roberts's second traveling companion was the jovial Captain Nelley of the 99th East Middlesex Regiment, who made himself very useful as an interpreter and was certainly the liveliest of the small group of adventurers. A third member, whom Roberts met in Cairo, later joined the expedition;

Roberts never revealed the identity of this mysterious Mr. A. The group was completed by Ismail, a young Egyptian converted to Christianity, hired by the artist as his personal servant. After taking on provisions for four months and safely stowing away the letters of introduction addressed to the pasha of Egypt, Mohammed Ali, Roberts left Alexandria at dawn on the 27th. The next morning the party reached the village of Asfeh, on one of the arms of the Nile. They then transferred to a more spacious boat, heading for Sa el-Hagar, the ancient Sais. On the 29th the boat put in at Nikleh, where a fair was underway. In his journal, Roberts wrote that people were flocking to the village from all directions, bringing with them goods of some kind or flocks of sheep and goats. In the artist's eyes the surrounding region appeared to be very fertile, partly because of the numerous wells (saqiyah), whose operation was highly ingenious despite their bizarre appearance.

**From David Roberts's journal:**

*September 29 - The waters of the Nile are thick and muddy; the region is intensively cultivated and dotted with villages, usually surrounded by palm trees which, by contrast with the whiteness of the minarets, make a very picturesque sight. The corn fields are irrigated by wells from which water is raised with earthenware pitchers secured to a rope which winds round a wheel pulled by an ox or a camel.*

A Persian Wheel,
used in Raising Water from the Nile.

David Roberts, R.A. — L. Haghe lith.

35

# THE GIZA FERRY IN THE PORT OF CAIRO

Plate 5

*September 30–October 7, 1838*

After leaving the village of Nikleh and covering some more equally picturesque stages on their journey, Roberts and his traveling companions eventually came in sight of the Pyramids at around midday on the 30th, and a few hours later landed at Boulak, the port of Cairo.

After booking into a hotel and calling on the British ambassador, Roberts visited the city and its amazing monuments. He was particularly impressed by the mosque of Sultan Hassan, whose extremely elaborate decorations took his breath away.

On the 3rd he traveled to the Pyramids by donkey. At first sight they did not look particularly huge, but he changed his mind when it came to climbing them. In any event, as he wrote in his journal, he was far more impressed by the sight of the Sphinx.

On the 5th he explored the tombs of the Caliphs, many of which were ruined by that time or inhabited by paupers and beggars, in striking contrast with the splendor of the magnificent mosaic floors, the finely painted walls and the domes studded with mother-of-pearl and semi-precious stones.

Enthusiastic about all these sights but ever mindful of his organizational responsibilities, he managed in the meantime to charter a fishing boat complete with its eight-man crew and captain, and drastically cleared it of rats by sinking it in the shallows for a few days. Vanderhorst, Captain Nelley and Mr. A. were to follow him on a second craft.

On October 6, he finally embarked after proudly hoisting the Union Jack, but was forced to spend the night on board in the port of Boulak because of the unfavorable wind. The next day, while he waited for the mainsail yard to be replaced after a slight rigging incident, he passed the time by drawing the Giza ferry, with the Pyramids in the background.

**From David Roberts's journal:**

*October 1 - From the heights of the Alcazar or the Citadel there is a magnificent view of Cairo: below lies the city with its domes and minarets, then the suburb of Boulak and the labyrinth of the Nile, while the Pyramids of Giza and the mountains of Libya stand out on the horizon.*

# THE ENTRANCE TO A TOMB AT BENI HASAN

Plate 6

*October 8–11, 1838*

During the night of the 7th, Roberts had his first unpleasant encounter with the local mosquitos, as a result of which he could not sleep a wink; unfortunately, he would have to get used to their company. The first few days of the trip were totally windless, so the crew had to man the oars most of the time.

The surrounding countryside passed slowly by with a continuous range of hills, and the monotony of the cornfields was only broken up here and there by poor villages of sun-dried mud or thick groves of date-laden palm trees. On the morning of the 9th, the boat landed at Beni Suef, where a market was in full swing. Roberts, always interested in details and anxious to see as much as possible, mingled with the crowds. The women, wearing ankle-length indigo blue cotton dresses, carried baskets full of fruit or cages of pigeons on their heads, while the men drove flocks of sheep and goats in front of them. All this formed a very picturesque setting, which he enjoyed very much.

The next day the boat put in at Sheikly, the ancient Cynopolis, where the sand dunes reached down to the banks of the great river. In order to stretch his legs, the artist decided to continue on foot to nearby Onaseh. During his walk he noticed that the local people did not bury their dead (probably because the tombs would have been flooded when the Nile periodically bursted its banks) but laid the bodies in small niches of unfired bricks that were soon damaged by the elements, with the result that macabre heaps of whitened skeletons, wrapped in the remains of their burial garments, were scattered all around.

Roberts spent the night at Minieh (present el-Minya), in the middle of which stood the ruins of an attractive mosque with marble columns. The next day the voyage continued, amid magnificent scenery, to Beni Hasan, where Roberts sketched the ancient ruins. The rock tombs of this district are named after an Arab tribe which occupied a number of neighboring villages, now abandoned and ruined.

The necropolis was excavated during the Middle Kingdom, and is considered to be of great interest, not only for its architecture but also for the splendid scenes of domestic life that decorate the tomb walls. The sepulchre illustrated by Roberts is that of the monarch Ammenemes, the front of which presents two interesting proto-Doric pillars.

**From David Roberts's journal:**

*October 11 - The main tomb has two Doric columns on the façade, and is entirely covered with hieroglyphics; inside, in a niche, are the remains of a large statue and two smaller ones, carved in the living rock. Other tombs are excavated in the rock walls that rise above the left bank of the Nile; nearly all of them are aligned at the same height. Each one has a well or a deep cavity which is perpendicular to the floor or slopes steeply.*

Entrance to the Caves of Beni Hassan.                    David Roberts R.A. Lefferts lith.

# SIOUT

Plate 7

October 11–13, 1838

*A*fter spending
a few hours at Beni Hasan,
Roberts set off for el-Sheik
Ibadah, the ancient Antinoe.
However, he was greatly
disappointed, as hardly a trace
remained of the glorious relics
described some years earlier by
other travelers. Here and there a
few columns still stood amid
rubble and piles of soil, but no
trace remained of the marble
triumphal arches of the Roman
period, which had almost
certainly been dismantled by the
local people to make lime.
Roberts consoled himself by
buying some ancient coins very
cheaply. His interest in
collecting coins is often
mentioned in his journal, where
he meticulously listed similar
purchases made in numerous
places.
On the 12th, the boat put in at
Manfalut, a declining town
whose bazaar provided six
chickens for the galley. The next
morning the expedition reached
Siout, known in ancient times
as Sauti, and now as Asyut. In
the past, the town had amassed
great wealth because of its
favorable position at the center
of a huge fertile plain, but
Roberts remarked that, as
elsewhere, little remained of the
ancient monuments but a few
heaps of rubble and some burial
areas.

**From David Roberts's journal:**

*October 13 - Much of the land is flooded, but the gardens surrounding Siout are very beautiful: palm trees, willows, sycamores, acacias and pomegranates grow in profusion. The town stands higher than the countryside around it; it is surrounded by embankments and reached by crossing a bridge formed by numerous arches. Last night someone stole the clothes and shoes of Ismail, who sleeps outside my cabin, but I am sure he will apply to me for compensation at the end of the journey.*

# THE MINARET OF THE GREAT MOSQUE AT SIOUT

Plate 8

*October 13, 1838*

**S**iout was once the center of the worship of Upuauet, the war god in the form of a desert wolf or lycaon, thus its Greek name of Lycopolis. It was the birthplace of neo-Platonic philosopher Plotinus in the 2nd century BC, and was later known as the city where the Holy Family stayed when they had to flee to Egypt to escape Herod's persecution. Converted to Christianity in the 4th century, it is still one of the largest Coptic centers in Egypt, although it also has a major Islamic university. Roberts described it as the largest city he encountered after leaving Cairo; a prosperous, well-kept town with numerous bazaars offering all sorts of goods. The solemnity of the merchants seemed rather absurd to him, however, because of their evident reluctance to take their chabouks (*a kind of long pipe*) out of their mouths to answer his questions. This and similar comments, which are by no means infrequent in his journal, give a faithful picture of the difficulties sometimes encountered by Roberts, although he often proved quite adaptable, in his contacts with such very different ways of life from his own. In any case, any misunderstandings must have been mutual.

Though puzzled by certain attitudes, the Scottish artist was genuinely fascinated by Islamic architecture, and unhesitatingly pronounced that the most outstanding monument in Siout was the Great Mosque, with its soaring minaret, which he lost no time in sketching.

After visiting the capital, Roberts walked to the rock necropolis, famous for the great tombs excavated halfway up a tall rock face. Though impressed by the magnificent tombs, the Scotsman could not conceal his irritation at the sight of evident traces left by mummy seekers who, during their sacrilegious operations, had scattered mutilated, shriveled human remains all around. This profanation was due to the widespread use of parts of mummies by Arab and European apothecaries from the Middle Ages onwards to prepare remedies that were popularly believed to have miracle-working properties. In pharmacological use this fashion reached its height in the 17th century, disappearing entirely around the turn of the 18th century, but mummies were still used in esoteric practices until the early decades of the 20th century. Needless to say, the damage caused by the tomb robbers in their frenetic excavations represents an incalculable loss to archaeology.

43

# THE TEMPLE OF DENDERA AND THE SO-CALLED TYPHONIUM

Plate 9

*October 14–20, 1838*

As mentioned in the Introduction, Roberts had planned his journey carefully in order to minimize the number of stops made and consequently the expense. He had decided to reach Abu Simbel as soon as possible, then sail back down the Nile to Cairo and begin the sketches, watercolors and oils that he would complete when he returned home. On the outward trip he therefore stopped only as long as absolutely necessary at the main archaeological sites, combining these stops (with laudable thrift) with the practical requirements of the expedition. While he measured façades, columns, funeral chambers and statues and recorded his data and personal impressions in his notebook, the crew restocked the galley and attended to the numerous other tasks required to ensure the success of the expedition.

At this stage, Roberts preferred merely to observe the spectacular remains of the pharaohs' Egypt, though with a technical eye, as if he wished to drink in the atmosphere of the extraordinary land he had long dreamed of before tackling the difficult task he had set himself. Only when he became accustomed to all this grandeur did he intend to commit the shapes and colors to paper. In fact, as can be seen from the pages of his journal, during the first weeks of the trip, until

Abu Simbel, Roberts produced very few complete drawings; he preferred sketches, details, perspective studies and the inevitable measurements. The only exceptions are views of some minor sites at which he decided not to stop on the return journey, and a few other lithographs mentioned in the journal, perhaps painted when he had more time to spare. However, it is reasonable to assume that in some cases he was carried away by enthusiasm, as in the case of this view of the Temple of Dendera and the adjacent Typhonium. Five days after leaving Siout on the 14th, Roberts reached the famous sanctuary of Hathor, following stops at Abutig, Antæopolis (where he saw a magnificent sunset over the ruins of the Roman amphitheater), el-Maragha, whose sheik welcomed him with great honors, and Girgah. On the 18th, while the boat was underway, he saw a group of huge crocodiles sniffing the morning air on a sandbank; they did not seem to be at all disturbed even by the rifle shots fired at them by the crew. Although the imposing ruins of Dendera had greatly impressed Roberts, he was plunged into a state of melancholic prostration at the thought of the transience of earthly things.

**From David Roberts's journal:**

*October 19 - I rose at dawn and betook myself to the ruins of Dendera accompanied by Captain Nelley, who acted as my assistant while I took measurements. On entering the temple I was amazed to see the marvellous state of preservation of the entire structure (with the sole exception of the points where it has been damaged intentionally) and the immense amount of work since the surface is covered with hieroglyphics, both inside and out. To the north-west stands the Typhonium, named after the figures of Typhon which appear frequently there.*

General View of The Ruins of Luxor from the Nile — David Roberts R A 1838

**From David Roberts's journal:**

*October 23 - The air is so pure and the plain on which it stands so large, that it is impossible to realise the size of the temple until you are really close to it; only the contrast with the homes that now surround the structures enables their majesty to be fully appreciated. The main columns, whose circumference is 30 feet, give some idea of the proportions of the complex; the capitals, carved to the shape of lotus flowers, must have a maximum circumference of 30 feet.*

# The Temple of Luxor
## seen from the Nile

Plate 10

*October 20–23, 1838*

Roberts reached Dendera on October 19 and set off again the next day, after completing a view of the temple and eating a good lunch. On the morning of Sunday the 21st, the two boats tied up near Goorna, a small village where visitors to ancient Thebes could spend the night and buy food and fresh water. The adventurous party wasted no time, but hired donkeys and set off for the great Theban necropolises that stretch along the west bank of the Nile. Here, in the plain dominated by the Theban Heights, the mountain sacred to the goddess Mertseger (She who loves Silence), stand the eternal resting places of pharaohs and royal brides, princes and princesses, officials and courtiers. The artist was particularly struck by the impressive appearance of what is known as the Memnonium, the funeral temple of Rameses II, in which lay the remains of the huge monolithic statue of the sovereign.

On the way back to the boats, various local inhabitants came to meet the newcomers, offering to sell them a number of exceptionally well preserved ancient mummies. On Monday morning the party visited the Valley of the Kings, where a number of unfinished tombs enabled Roberts to study the construction techniques and the methods used by the decorators. A few laconic words written in his faithful journal indicate that the evening reserved a pleasant surprise for the tired traveling companions: a performance by some young dancers, who were "very elegant and graceful." The Scotsman particularly liked a very tall girl with ebony skin, whose perfect features seemed the most expressive he had ever seen in his life. In his descriptions of the dancers and the women he had admired in Egypt in general, Roberts is certainly the most reserved of his contemporaries; perhaps he censored his notes later so as not to scandalize his daughter, or perhaps the modest Christine cut certain passages of her own initiative when recopying her father's memories.

On the 23rd, the moment finally came to visit the spectacular ruins of Luxor, which took the artist's breath away; the notes in his journal clearly indicate that the dimensions of the complex almost obsessed poor Roberts, who spent hours measuring columns, capitals, reliefs and walls in a paroxysm of amazement and admiration.

View of Luxor, from the South-west

# THE TEMPLE OF LUXOR
## SEEN FROM THE SOUTHWEST

Plate 11

*October 23, 1838*

Luxor, now a flourishing tourist resort on the east bank of the Nile 450 miles south of Cairo, is universally famous for its majestic ruins, which were explored and described in detail as early as the period of Napoleon Bonaparte's expedition. Here, in the fertile plain that occupies a vast loop of the river, one of the greatest religious and political centers in the ancient world developed in the 2nd millennium BC: a city so rich and influential that at the height of its glory it had the astonishing population of half a million inhabitants.

by the regional capital. The god Amun, associated with Mut and Khonsu in the Theban Triad, was worshipped with great ceremony in the huge metropolis. The spiritual rule of the triad was imposed on every other town in the country by extensive proselytizing work carried out by the powerful priestly caste of the district. The Great Temple of Luxor was the main satellite of the huge sacred complex of Karnak, with which it was closely linked for reasons of worship and by architectural and ornamental characteristics due to the same

As a matter of fact, the present town is only part of ancient Thebes, several times capital of Egypt during the Middle and New Kingdoms, which developed from the original urban nucleus located near present-day Karnak, and rapidly grew until it included the area now occupied

historical events. Already greatly excited by the sanctuary of Luxor, Roberts described Karnak, where he arrived on the afternoon of October 23, in almost astonished tones, again emphasizing the formidable size of those temples that had survived the millennia.

# ASWAN AND THE
# ELEPHANTINE ISLAND

Plate 12

*October 24–29, 1838*

Roberts left Karnak on the afternoon of October 23, and reached Aswan six days later after calling at the places of greatest historical interest. On the 24th the artist first visited the picturesque ruins of Hermonthis, then stayed for a few hours at Esna to view the remains of the temple of Khnum. At dawn the next day he strolled on the plain around ancient Eilathia, surrounded by mighty walls, and on the 26th he decided to visit Edfu, whose temple interested him greatly because of its size and the supreme elegance of its bas-reliefs. On the 28th he was at Kom Ombo, where the ruins of the sanctuary dominated the lazy waters of the Nile like giants half-buried in the sand.

As usual, Roberts wrote detailed descriptions of each monument, but the pages of his journal are fascinating not so much for his architectural notes as for his brilliant landscape descriptions, which, in a few words describe sceneries, often with a wild beauty, that are now lost forever. For example, before reaching Edfu, he wrote, "About midway we found a sheik's tomb, in which were jars of water for the thirsty traveler. A lean hungry dog and two immense white eagles were gorging themselves on a dead camel, and they scarcely stopped when we approached them."

On the 27th, he spent the whole day on board, and wrote, "Scarcely a breath of wind. Crocodiles lie sunning themselves on the banks. The cooing of the wild pigeons, and the notes of numerous birds, are heard from the groves of palms, and the solitary crane stalks along by the river-side."

Aswan, called Syene by the Greeks, once famous for its granite quarries, is situated under the First Cataract of the Nile, where the great river branches, and is studded with a myriad of granite rocks and some larger islands. The entire area surrounding the present-day city was known in ancient times by the name of Yeb, or "Land of Elephants," perhaps because the Egyptians saw the huge animals there for the first time, or because of the fact that many of the rocks molded by the water resemble elephants; only later was the name restricted to the strategically located Elephantine Island and the town that developed there. Roberts was ferried there, but discovered with some disappointment that only a few slight traces of the ancient ruins remained.

General View of Essouan and the Island of Elephantine

*October 29 - On reaching Aswan we wandered among the ruins of the city, which stands on a rise overlooking the river. All that remains of it are a few brick walls, so after making a drawing of this section of the Nile, I crossed it to visit Elephantine Island. Here I found no sign of ancient temples apart from a few columns and heaps of rubble. However, I saw a solitary statue, and on examining the wall next the stream I found it composed of stones covered with hieroglyphics.*

# THE SO-CALLED HYPAETHRAL TEMPLE ON THE ISLE OF PHILAE

Plate 13

*November 1, 1838*

On the morning of November 30, after hiring a number of donkeys, Roberts and his tireless traveling companions set off southward in search of a boatman who could ferry them across to the Isle of Philae, the "pearl of Egypt," where pilgrims congregated in ancient times to pay homage to the mysterious, benign goddess Isis. The magnificent ruins of the great sanctuary still survived in all their splendor, and the artist was greatly impressed. The island, which he described as a corner of paradise in the midst of boundless desolation, somehow recalled the green land where he was born and the happy times of his youth, a pleasant sensation that he was never to forget. The time passed quickly as the four gentlemen roamed around the ancient walls, and the time to take their leave of this delightful spot came all too quickly. The next day, while preparations were being made for the crossing of the First Cataract, a messenger reached Aswan bearing an invitation from the bey himself. The lord of the district welcomed Roberts and Captain Nelley into his tent with great courtesy; as he offered them coffee and good tobacco he told them he had been ordered by the pasha to give them all possible assistance, but Roberts politely declined the courteous offer.

This answer was perhaps too hasty, because crossing the rapids with the two boats proved very laborious, and took up the whole of November 1. The artist therefore decided to spend the time available at Philae, where he drew what is known as the "Pharaoh's Bed," which he described as a "hypaethral temple" because it had no roof. In fact, the pavilion was erected by Trajan in AD 105 as a shelter for the sacred boat of Isis on which the statue of the goddess was carried during processions to the temples of southern Nubia. The elegant structure consists of a quadrangular kiosk formed by 14 columns united at the base by intercolumnar walls, mostly devoid of decoration. The capitals, no two of which are alike, are the floral type. The unusual cubes surmounting them were to have been carved with the effigy of Hathor. Though incomplete, the kiosk has become the very symbol of Philae because of its beauty, and still remains the best example of the taste and skill of Egyptian architecture in the Roman period. The monument became famous as the "Pharaoh's Bed" because it was wrongly believed in ancient times that the sovereigns of Egypt resided there during their visits to the great sanctuary.

**From David Roberts's journal:**

*October 30 - There are four temples on the island. The first I visited, with lotus-shaped capitals, is the southernmost one. It gives the impression of being unfinished. It is made of very fine sandstone, and the details of the decorations are so clear as to suggest that the stone cutters have only just finished work. I can hardly convince myself that I have seen a 2,000-year-old monument. We set off again, and at sunset we finally entered Nubia.*

# The Temple of Wadi Dabod

Plate 14

*November 2, 1838*

On the morning of Friday, November 2, Roberts and his traveling companions went ashore near Wadi Dabod, in a place where a small temple with very elegant proportions stood. Like many other Nubian sanctuaries it was never completed, as demonstrated by the fact that the two outer columns on the façade are unpolished. Their irregular surface and the roughly hewn capitals confirmed to the artist's eyes the supposition that Egyptian craftsmen carved the hieroglyphics and smaller details of the decoration after the various blocks of stone had been assembled in their correct positions.

The oldest part of the temple was built in the first half of the 3rd century BC by King Adikhalamani, who dedicated it to the god Amun; during the next century it was reconsecrated to the goddess Isis, and extended on various occasions by Ptolemy VI and Ptolemy VIII. The construction of the left wing and the addition of the façade, with its four great columns, were ordered by Roman emperors Augustus and Tiberius, who were portrayed with the attributes of the ancient pharaohs on the walls built up to halfway up the intercolumniations.

As in the case of the more famous temples of Abu Simbel and Philae, the small temple of Wadi Dabod also risked being submerged by the waters of Lake Nasser when the Great Aswan Dam was built, but was saved by the intervention of UNESCO; it was dismantled between 1960 and 1961, and the pieces were temporarily stored. Later, the Egyptian government donated them to Spain in gratitude for that country's help during the salvage operations, and the monument was reconstructed in 1968 on a hill not far from Madrid, in the Parque de la Montaña.

After taking notes and drawing the site, Roberts walked on to Wadi Kardassy, where he found a temple similar to the one he had just seen; however, as sunset was imminent he decided to postpone a more detailed visit until his return.

*Temple at Wady Dabod, Nubia.*

**From David Roberts's journal:**

*November 22 - This morning we put in at Wadi Dabod, where a small unfinished temple stands. In the* adytum *there is a red granite votive chapel which probably contained the statue of Isis; the type of decoration suggests that it is much older than the temple.*

**From David Roberts's journal:**

*November 4 - Today we stopped below the small temple of Dandour. The building, which stands just under the line of the Tropic, is formed by a portico with two columns on the front, followed by two rooms and finally by the actual* cella. *Here there is a small stele, probably dedicated to Isis. The winged solar globe appears on the architrave, while the walls of the* pronaos *are decorated with the figures of Isis and Osiris offering sacrifices.*

# THE TEMPLE OF DANDOUR

<u>Plate 15</u>

*November 3–4, 1838*

*A*fter a few hours at Kalabsha, a village on the west bank of the Nile near which stood a magnificent temple, Roberts spent the night of November 3 on board, and went ashore near Dandour at daybreak. As he himself admitted, the small temple in this area might appear trivial by comparison with the grandiose buildings he had seen up to this point. Nevertheless, the monument possessed an intrinsic historical value as it was built by Augustus in honor of the local divinities Peteese and Pihor. Augustus, who was strongly attracted by Egyptian culture, always considered Egypt as his private possession, and this preference (shared by many of his successors) led to a fashion based on pharaonic art

in Rome. Even after his death, one of the characteristic features of Roman rule in Egypt was that local building styles continued to be used. Threatened by the waters of Lake Nasser, the Temple of Dandour was dismantled in 1963 on the initiative of UNESCO, and donated by Egypt to the United States. It is now on view in a special room of the Metropolitan Museum of Art in New York. The presence in this plate of a number of people intent on measuring the temple façade is interesting; the fact that one of them is wearing European dress suggests that Roberts could not resist the temptation of depicting himself, the loyal Ismail and some members of the crew.

# THE TEMPLE OF WADI SABOUA

Plate 16

*November 5–6, 1838*

On the night of November 4, the boat passed alongside the temples of Gyrshe and Dakke, and by dawn was close to the island of Derar, which Roberts described as being intensively cultivated. The rising sun shone down on stretches of gleaming white sand, in the middle of which, at a certain point, the outline of the Temple of Offalina stood out. This place is also known by the name of Maharraqa. The Scottish artist went ashore for as long as necessary to visit the great complex, which greatly impressed him, and returned on board in the early afternoon. The next day the heat was oppressive, and the total absence of wind slowed the progress of the boat, with the result that the majestic ruins of Wadi Saboua did not appear on the horizon until the early hours of November 6. The temple, which Roberts much admired, met the same fate as nearly all the other Nubian monuments; it was dismantled into great numbered blocks and was later rebuilt some two and half miles from its original location in a place called New Sabu, on the banks of the great reservoir. The sacred building was erected by Rameses II and consecrated to Amun and Ra-Harakhti, the supreme divinities of Egypt under Rameses; the founder also had himself worshipped, with the result that the temple was known as "The House of Rameses-Meryamun in the dominion of Amun." That is why the sphinxes and statues erected in front of the pylon bore the features of the deified sovereign. In his journal, Roberts wrote that the most spectacular feature of the complex was the long dromos, a kind of avenue lined with sphinxes and preceded by two huge statues of the pharaoh, which led to the temple. It was the sphinxes that suggested to the local people the modern name given to the site, namely Valley of Lions. This plate is of great historical value, as most of these sculptures have sadly been lost.

Approach to the Temple of Wady Saboua. Nubia

**From David Roberts's journal:**

*November 6 - Yesterday the thermometer read 96.8°F in the shade, and there was not a breath of wind. After sunset a slight breeze rose, and this morning we woke not far from Wadi Saboua. The ruins of the temple lie on the west bank of the Nile, 1,485 feet from the river, in the middle of what must once have been a fertile plain. Now great heaps of sand have covered it, burying the portico of the temple; a few stunted bushes are the only signs of plant life, and there is not a single hut in sight.*

# THE TEMPLE OF WADI SABOUA
## SEEN FROM THE COURTYARD

Plate 17

*November 6, 1838*

*The entrance to the temple proper consists of a reddish sandstone pylon 60 feet tall, once preceded by two huge statues of Rameses II, only one of which is still in its original place. The central portal, decorated with bas-reliefs portraying the sovereign offering sacrifices to the gods, leads to the courtyard, bounded on two sides by porticoes with five pillars each; a huge statue of the pharaoh rests on each pillar. The bas-reliefs carved on the walls portray the usual scenes of offerings.*
*From the courtyard a staircase leads to a narrow terrace onto which opens the portal leading to the main hall; this was converted into a church in the Christian era after many of the reliefs had been covered with frescoes. This large hall, only partly roofed by a ceiling supported by pillars, is followed by a room built crosswise to it, entirely excavated in the rock, which linked to various other rooms.*
*The numerous reliefs show*

*Rameses II making offerings to the gods and to his own deified image. In the back wall there are three chapels; the central chapel was the actual naos. Here, some of the images decorating the walls represent the pharaoh taking flowers to Ra-Harakhti's solar boat, decorated with hawks' heads, and to Amun's, decorated with rams' heads. A niche contains the statues of the three divinities worshipped in the sanctuary, which were badly damaged by the early Christians.*
*When Roberts reached Wadi Saboua, the hypogean part could not be visited, as it was blocked by a great mass of sand that also partly obstructed the courtyard. He also noticed that the friable material with which the building was constructed was showing evident signs of erosion, and that many blocks were loose, perhaps because of earth tremors. In fact, when the sanctuary was reconstructed, it required extensive restoration work.*

**From David Roberts's journal:**

*November 6 - Much of the temple is buried under the sand, the smooth surface of which is only broken by the trails left by snakes and the tiny tracks of a few lizards. The words of the Biblical prophecy really seem to have come wholly true, "I will make the land of Egypt utterly waste and desolate, from Migdol to Syene and even unto the border of Ethiopia."*

*Temple of Wady Saboua, Nubia*

# TWO COLOSSAL STATUES
# IN THE TEMPLE OF WADI SABOUA

Plate 18

*November 6, 1838*

*T*wo enormous statues stood guard in front of the pylon, terminating the long access dromos to the temple, and two more, portraying Rameses II with the headgear and emblems of the god Osiris, stood at the start of the avenue. Only the Colossus, which Roberts portrayed standing, now survives; the others have been stolen or destroyed. The statue portrays the sovereign with the symbol of Amun-Ra, a long stick that ends in a ram's head surmounted by the solar disk and the uraeus, the sacred cobra that symbolized light and sovereignty. Rameses is wearing the Nubian hairstyle of fine plaits, with a narrow band around his head and the uraeus on his forehead. The Temple of Wadi Saboua is the only Nubian sanctuary whose dromos has survived, though only in part. Before the temple was rebuilt in an area 198 feet higher than the original site, this avenue led directly from the bank of the Nile to the sanctuary. Roberts stayed at Wadi Saboua all day on November 6, and set off the next morning for Abu Simbel after measuring and drawing properly the ruins of the sanctuary. On several occasions the Scotsman wrote of how much he enjoyed the long hours spent sailing down the great river, and not only because of the splendid

landscape; he was also exceedingly proud of leading a crew of such skilled men. He often observed the bright Union Jack fluttering from the mast with equal pleasure, especially when they passed other vessels flying weatherworn flags or the crescent of the pasha of Egypt.

Colossus in front of Temple of Wady Seboua, Nubia.                                         David Roberts

**From David Roberts's journal:**

*November 9 - This morning I finally reached Abu Simbel, the great temple excavated in rock that has so often been described. Carved on the mountain face are four colossal human figures in a seated position.*

# THE ARRIVAL AT THE TEMPLES OF ABU SIMBEL

Plate 19

*November 7–9, 1838*

On the morning of November 7, the two boats moored near Kosocko, a pleasant looking town where it was decided to spend the entire day. The rest was very welcome after such a long navigation, and Roberts spent the time observing local customs with his usual interest. At sunset the crew went back on board, and a few hours later, Hassaia and Derr were already receding into the distance.

In the early hours of the next morning the Scottish artist viewed the magnificent ruins of the fortress of Ibrim, which he decided to examine with greater attention on the return trip as the destination of his voyage was now only a few miles away.

Abu Simbel appeared on the horizon as night was falling, and only the increasing darkness could delay the long-awaited moment. After a few hours' sleep, David Roberts finally arrived in front of the two huge temples excavated in the rock: it was dawn on Friday, November 9, 1838.

Abu Simbel had been discovered only 25 years earlier, in March 1813, by famous Swiss explorer Johann Ludwig Burckhardt, but its fame had already spread far and wide. Englishman William John Bankes and Italian Giovanni Finati, attracted by the description of the fabulous site, had managed to enter the smaller temple, dedicated to Hathor and Queen Nefertari, in 1815, but were unable to shift the great mass of sand that obstructed the façade of the large temple. All they could see of it was the bust of one of the four great statues of Rameses II. After a similarly fruitless attempt by Piedmontese Consul Drovetti, Giovanni Battista Belzoni finally managed to enter the temple on August 1, 1817 after spending more than a month in the difficult undertaking of removing the sand.

When Roberts reached the spot, the gorge that separated the two rock temples was still partly blocked by a great sand dune that reached down to the waters of the Nile, but the two monuments were mostly visible. Roberts was the first to depict them correctly in all their splendor, with his usual meticulous attention to architectural proportions and details.

**From David Roberts's journal:**

*November 9 - It is appalling to see these masterpieces of ancient art not only massacred by souvenir hunters but actually covered with the signatures of every Tomkins, Smith and Hopkins. One of the hands of the best preserved colossus has been literally destroyed by these vandals who, not content with having taken a finger of the great statue as a souvenir of their deplorable exploit, have then had the gall to carve their stupid names on the very forehead of the god.*

# The Great Temple of Abu Simbel

Plate 20

*November 9, 1838*

*R*oberts described Abu Simbel as "the monument which alone makes the trip to Nubia worthwhile." The colossi were in an exceptionally good state of preservation, undoubtedly due to the long period they had spent buried in the sand, which sheltered them from the ravages of time and the elements. However, in the few years that had elapsed since their discovery, the stupidity of Western travelers had already left its indelible mark; dozens of signatures carved in the stone ruined their solemnity, and the same vandals had removed numerous fragments to show off as souvenirs on their return home. Disgusted at the sight of this vandalism, Roberts expressed the hope that the sand would providentially return to cover the magnificent sanctuary. It is therefore curious, to say the least, that in the lithograph the signature of none other than Roberts himself appears right on the instep of the first colossus. However, the blame for this embarrassing incident can be attributed to Louis Haghe, who probably thought that the artist would be pleased if he added this unfortunate detail. This hypothesis is borne out by the fact that the signature is followed by the initials R.A. (Royal Academician), which Roberts would not have added himself since he did not actually become a member of the Royal Academy until two years after his return home.

# THE COLOSSI OF RAMESES II AT ABU SIMBEL

<u>Plate 21</u>

*November 9, 1838*

*E*ven today, the temple's gigantic proportions are astonishing: its façade is 125 feet wide and 100 feet high, the equivalent of a modern nine-storey building. The four statues, which stand over 65 feet tall, finely reproduce the features of the sovereign, adorned with the crowns of Upper and Lower Egypt and the cobra symbol, the uraeus, *the attribute of Osiris. From the purely static point of view the architects of the period solved the serious problem of the stability of the complex by using the four colossi as load-bearing pillars, against which the enormous load of the rock mass behind was equally distributed. A multitude of slaves under the orders of head sculptor Pyay, whose name is recalled in an inscription, completed the elaborate front of the temple, framed by a convex molding called a torus, surmounted by a cornice with* uraei, *above which runs a high-relief strip depicting twenty-two seated baboons, each over eight feet tall. Below the torus runs a molding carved with dedicatory hieroglyphics, and further down, in a niche in the middle of the façade, is the great statue portraying Ra-Harakhti with a*

*sparrow hawk's head. As the god rests his right hand on the scepter with the head of the jackal (User) and his left on the scepter with the figure of Maat, goddess of truth and justice, the three figures form the name User-Maat-Ra, adopted by the pharaoh when he ascended to the throne. At the sides, two large bas-reliefs portray the features of Rameses II. Between the legs of each colossus stand other smaller statues that portray the members of the royal family; there are pictures of black and Asian prisoners on the plinth and on the sides of the chairs. The work of stone masons and sculptors was followed by that of painters, but time and the incessant ravages of wind and sand have entirely cancelled out what at the time of Rameses must have been a very rich range of colors. The ruthless work of nature attacked the temple even in ancient times; in fact, the most serious damage was caused by earth tremors. One of the colossi, the third from the left, was repaired in the time of Pharaoh Sethi II, around 1200 BC, while the upper part of the second, which fell during the 34th year of Rameses' reign, has lain on the ground ever since.*

**From David Roberts's journal:**

*November 9 - The beauty and size of the temple are not surpassed by any other Egyptian monument, even the Theban sanctuaries. If it is compared with the heads of Isis decorating the capitals of the Temple of Dendera, the most elaborate and best finished of the Egyptian temples, the poor goddess actually seems coarse. And to think that Dendera is far more recent than Abu Simbel!*

Front Elevation of the Great Temple of Aboosimbel - Nubia.

# THE INTERIOR OF THE GREAT TEMPLE AT ABU SIMBEL

Plate 22

*November 9, 1838*

The rock sanctuary of Abu Simbel symbolizes the boundless ambitions of the most powerful pharaoh of ancient Egypt. Dedicated in theory to the triad of divinities consisting of Amen-Ra, Harmakhis and Ptah, the temple was actually built to glorify over the centuries the name of its builder, Rameses II the Great, who reigned for 67 long years, from 1290 to 1224 BC. The images of the Pharaoh, repeated some hundred times on the façade and the walls of the several rooms, show him at various moments of his life: son, husband, proud father, victorious warrior and, finally, worshipped as a god on earth. However, it would be a mistake to consider Abu Simbel as the embodiment of a megalomaniac's dream, because Rameses II was actually a great sovereign, skilled diplomat and brilliant strategist whose self-deification was the last stage in a plan aimed at making his rule totally stable. From the architectural standpoint, the sanctuary is nothing other than the magnificent transposition of the architectural features of the classic Egyptian temple into the living rock.
Thus, while the façade was designed as a pylon, the succession of rooms built behind rather than above it involved the mammoth task of penetrating layers of sandstone. The experience of moving from the outside, flooded with blinding light, to the silent darkness of the pronaos, is an indescribable one that greatly moved the Scottish artist. The ceiling of the huge rectangular room, 60 feet long and 50 feet wide, is supported by eight pillars, 30 feet tall, arranged in two rows, on each of which rests a statue representing Osiris with the features of Rameses II.
The giants on the left wear the white crown of Upper Egypt, while those on the right wear the pschent (double crown); the hands crossed on the chest hold the heka (scepter) and the nekhaka (scourge), both symbols of power and royalty. A great vulture, the emblem of the goddess Nekhebet, protectress of Upper Egypt, is painted on the ceiling of the nave, while the ceilings of the aisles represent a starry sky. Most of the wall paintings illustrate scenes from the Battle of Kadesh, which victoriously concluded the pharaoh's military campaign against the Hittites in the fifth year of his reign. Many scenes show the sovereign sacrificing prisoners to the gods, and the bas-relief that shows the pharaoh standing in his war chariot seizing his bow is an absolute masterpiece.
Six more rooms, in which the votive offerings were placed, surround this room to the right and left. The pronaos is followed by a second hypostyle room supported by four square pillars on which pictures of the pharaoh seated in front of various divinities are painted. Note the blunder made in the dating of the plate by Haghe or one of his assistants; the day and month are correct, but the year is wrong.

# THE NAOS OF THE GREAT TEMPLE AT ABU SIMBEL

Plate 23

*November 10, 1838*

The sacrarium, the most remote and secret part of the temple, is situated 215 feet from the entrance, in the heart of the mountain. In this small room, which measures 13 feet wide and just over 23 feet deep, stand the statues of Amun-Ra, Harmakhis, Ptah and Rameses II. Careful observation of the arrangement of the temple revealed as early as the 19th century that the complex was built in accordance with a precise plan, in which nothing was left to chance. Twice a year, at the solstices, a ray of sunlight penetrates the corridor separating the entrance from the naos at 5:58 a.m. and floods the left shoulder of Amun-Ra with light. A few moments later, having touched the image of the sovereign, it concentrates on Harmakhis. The "sun miracle" lasts for around 20 minutes. It is very significant that the statue of the last divinity is never touched by the sunbeam, as Ptah was the Lord of Darkness. However, the fascination of Abu Simbel is not limited only to this ingenious system. In order to understand the significance of the Nubian temple fully, it should be remembered that this was the sanctuary in which Rameses II decided to deify himself. The pharaoh originally worshipped Horus, son of Isis and Osiris and Lord of Meha;

he later began to identify with the god himself, and decided to excavate a temple in the same mountain of Meha, now called Abu Simbel. The gradual illumination of the three divinities takes place between February 10 and March 1, and from October 10 through 30. On February 21 and October 21 the first rays of the sun are exactly on the axis of the temple; the second date corresponds to the first jubilee, celebrated after 30 years of Ramses II's reign. Here, Rameses II is identified with a solar divinity the equal of Amun-Ra and Harmakhis. When it became necessary to dismantle the temples of Abu Simbel and rebuild them in a higher position to save them from the waters of the artificial Lake Nasser, special attention was paid to the orientation of the main sanctuary so that the "miracle of the sun" could still take place. The work began in spring 1964 under the sponsorship of UNESCO, and was completed four years later. The Great Temple was cut into 807 blocks with an average weight of 20 tons each and reassembled on a huge reinforced concrete skeleton. The great illumination event was repeated in February 1969, taking place just as it did 3,000 years earlier, and continues to this day.

**From David Roberts's journal:**

*November 9 - In the* cella *there are four plaster-covered, painted deities; opposite them stand the remains of an altar, also excavated in the living rock. The corners are intact and regular, but the top is damaged. It is the only thing of the kind I have seen so far, and it is truly fascinating. Some 24 inches in front of the altar there are grooves and holes in the walls on both sides, perhaps left by a kind of gate that prevented worshippers from entering the room.*

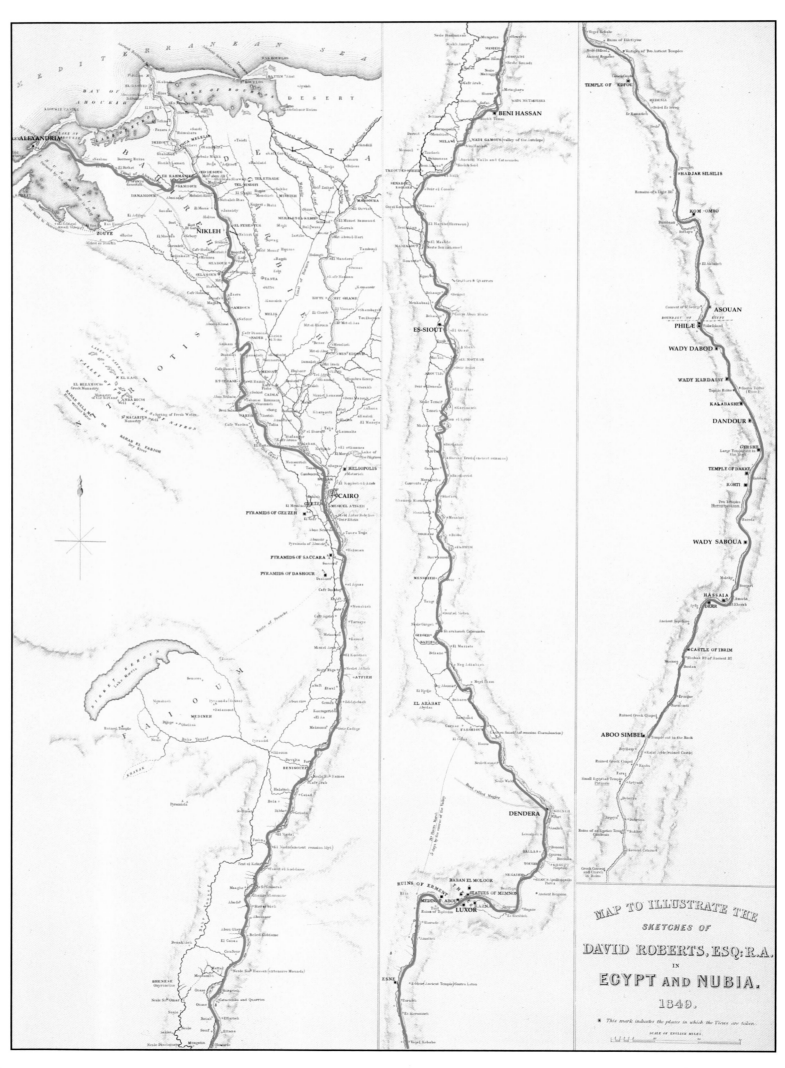

MAP TO ILLUSTRATE THE
SKETCHES OF
DAVID ROBERTS, ESQ: R.A.
IN
EGYPT AND NUBIA.
1849.

* *This mark indicates the places in which the Views are taken.*

SCALE OF ENGLISH MILES.

# EGYPT & NUBIA

FROM DRAWINGS MADE ON THE SPOT

David Roberts R.A.

WITH HISTORICAL DESCRIPTIONS BY

WILLIAM BROCKEDON, F.R.S.

LITHOGRAPHED BY

LOUIS HAGHE.

VOL. I.

Entrance to the Great Temple of Aboo Simbel, Nubia.

LONDON. F. G. MOON, 20, THREADNEEDLE STREET.

PUBLISHER IN ORDINARY TO HER MAJESTY.

MDCCCXLVI.

# The Nile in the vicinity of the Fortress of Ibrim

Plate 24

*November 11–12, 1838*

*A*bu Simbel, 530 miles from Cairo, was usually the southernmost point reached by European travelers of the day, and Roberts was no exception. While the artist was busy with his pencils and watercolors, the other members of the expedition continued as far as Wadi Halfa to see the Second Cataract of the Nile; however, their description, far from interesting him, persuaded him to go no further. He decided that it would be far more convenient to finish his last drawings (which demonstrate his great preference for the Great Temple over the Sanctuary of Hathor and Nefertari, inhabited by swarms of bats and other "beasties") and immediately commence the return journey. On November 11, as evening fell, the two boats began to descend the river, and a few hours later tied up near the Fortress of Ibrim. These few notes written by the author reveal the feeling of relief felt by the entire party at that change of horizon: "Thank God our vessel's prow now faces the north and civilisation."

For weeks Roberts and the others had borne the most intolerable heat, eaten dates and drunk brackish water, suffered from mosquito and horsefly bites and often slept in uncomfortable conditions, wrapped in their jackets to protect themselves against the damp of the night, so the mere thought of the comforts of Cairo must have seemed like heaven.

**From David Roberts's journal:**

*November 11 - The rubble lies in layers, and it seems clear that the village which grew up around the fortress was built on the ruins of the previous ones. The fortress must have been very powerful and well defended; some ruins here and there indicate its very remote origin.*

# The Fortress of Ibrim

Plate 25

*November 12, 1838*

*A*fter waking
at sunrise, Roberts spent the
early hours of the 12th drawing.
The ruins of the Fortress
of Ibrim, which stood alone
on a tall promontory jutting
out over the river, made a very
attractive sight, and to some
extent recalled the Moorish
castles he had visited during
his journey to Spain.
The origins of the fortress date
back to the period of Roman
rule, when the place was known
as Primis and occupied one
of the most strategically
important positions in all
Nubia, standing guard over
the traffic along the Nile.
In the 16th century the fortress
was occupied by the Bosnian
contingent sent by Sultan Selim I
to conquer the region; it was
held in 1812 by the Mamluks
fleeing from the army of
Mohammed Ali's son Ibrahim,
but was retaken and destroyed
by him. Sadly, the majestic ruins
of the fortress are now
submerged by the waters
of Lake Nasser, so that Roberts's
work has a unique historical
value. From this point on the
artist makes no explicit mention
of his traveling companions,
so it is probable that Captain
Nelley, Mr. V. and Mr. A.
decided to return directly
to Cairo.

# THE TEMPLE OF AMADA AT HASSAYA

Plate 26

*November 12–13 1838*

*During the night the boat reached Derr, the capital of Nubia, which Roberts described as a large city whose houses were certainly better built and more attractive than those of Lower Egypt. Oddly, the walls of the buildings sloped inwards, so that the houses were shaped like truncated pyramids. Roberts was particularly impressed by a huge sycamore that stood right in the middle of the capital. He also visited the small rock temple located nearby, but did not draw it,*

*hovels; the pronaos was surmounted by the unwieldy bulk of a mud and straw dome, almost certainly built when the temple was converted into a Christian church. The sanctuary, which was founded by Thutmoses III and continued by Amenhotep II in the 15th century BC, is not particularly large, but its proportions are very elegant and it is entirely covered with reliefs of exquisite workmanship. During the campaign to save the Nubian monuments,*

*certainly because it must have seemed very modest by comparison with Abu Simbel. The next day he visited the Sanctuary of Amada, near Hassaya. The building was partly buried by sand and surrounded by various ruined*

*the Temple of Amada was entirely enclosed in a steel and cement framework weighing 990 tons and moved to its new site, nearly two miles away and 200 feet higher, by a three-rail rack railway built expressly for this purpose.*

*November 13 – The temple is still intact, and its walls, like those of the two rooms communicating with it, are covered with tiny hieroglyphics of exquisite workmanship, carved with far greater expertise than those generally seen in similar buildings. Their colours are bright, and in almost perfect condition.*

# THE TEMPLE OF WADI MAHARRAKA

Plate 27

*November 14, 1838*

*After spending the whole night sailing down the river, in the early hours of November 14, Roberts came in sight of the Temple of Maharraka, which he had already visited ten days earlier. The small building was in an advanced state of disrepair, but 14 of the 16 columns in the inner courtyard were still standing. Because of the roughly hewn capitals and almost total absence of wall decorations, the artist easily deduced that the building, like most of the Nubian temples, had remained unfinished because of the spread of Christianity in the region; in addition, the numerous frescoes depicting Biblical subjects that were still visible clearly demonstrated that the sanctuary, originally dedicated to Isis and Serapis, had been converted into a church. The temple, of which all that remains is the hypostyle room illustrated by Roberts, stood in the ancient Hierasykaminos (City of the Sacred Sycamore), which marked the southernmost border of the Roman Empire from 23 BC to AD 297.*

*The spiral staircase in the north east corner leading to the portico roof constitutes a unique exception in Egyptian architecture, and can only be explained by the fact that the temple was almost certainly designed by a Roman architect.*

*The Temple of Maharraka, restored in 1908, was dismantled during the campaign to save the Nubian monuments and rebuilt at New Saboua. After the construction of the Great Aswan Dam, inaugurated on January 15, 1971, no less than 20 temples standing on the banks of the Nile between the First and Second Cataracts ran the risk of being submerged by the waters of the great artificial Lake Nasser. In order to save them, UNESCO devised one of the most extraordinary international salvage programs ever undertaken to preserve architectural and art treasures, which concluded with the recovery of most of the sanctuaries in the preservation areas. Five of the minor temples were donated by Egypt to countries that had generously participated in the huge project (the United States, the Netherlands, Germany, Italy and Spain) and reconstructed in those countries. The main ones were assembled in three different areas: New Kalabsha, where the rock temple of Beit el-Wali is also located, New Saboua and New Amada. However, despite these mammoth efforts, not all the Nubian monuments could be saved, and some of them lie forever beneath the waters of the Nile.*

David Roberts R.A. _ L. Haghe, lith.

Nubian Women at Kortie, on the Nile

# Nubian women at Korti

Plate 28

*November 14, 1838*

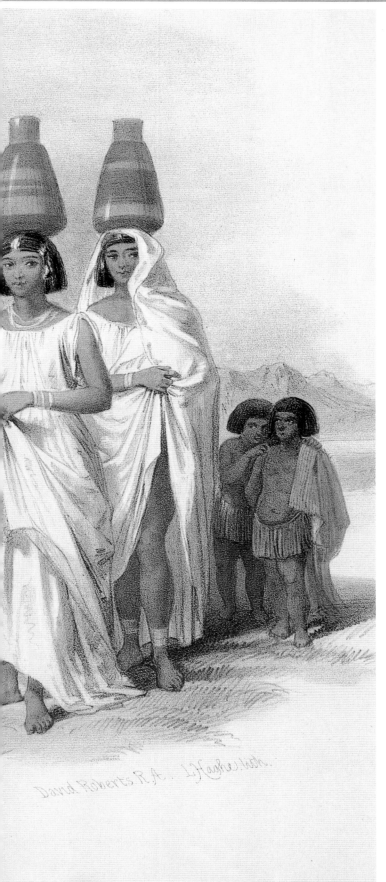

*This lithograph, generally omitted from modern reproductions of Roberts's works as no monument appears in it, provides insight into the tastes of the period in which he lived and worked, which were already quite chaste, but not yet fiercely repressed by Victorian morality. The scene shows young Nubian women carrying water near Korti, a village where the boat tied up on the afternoon of November 14; however, the author pays more attention to the beauty of the girls than to local customs.*

*Roberts was evidently equally susceptible to the charms of the exotic and the charms of women, and in this rare case his temperament as a man and an artist led him to take an unaccustomed liberty. Many other contemporary artists, like Emile Prisse d'Avennes, were dazzled by the sinuous grace of the local girls, especially the most scantily clad, who constituted an excellent subject in the name of art. This subject could also be enjoyed without embarrassment by the purchaser of the work, on the pretext of learned ethnological interest.*

*Various entries in Roberts's journal mention the beauty of the local women with great enthusiasm; it is a pity that these accounts were censored in several places by the prudish Christine, who evidently considered certain passages too licentious to be made public, as she thought they might show her famous father in a dubious light. This is a pity, because the portrait of the artist would certainly have gained in humanity and become less antiseptic if these passages had been presented in their entirety.*

# A GROUP OF ABYSSINIAN SLAVES AT KORTI

Plate 29

*November 14, 1838*

*Abyssinian Slaves resting at Korti — Nubia*

N ear Korti, Roberts came upon a group of Abyssinian slaves, mostly young women, who were waiting in the shade of a few stunted palm trees to be taken to the Cairo market. The girl in the middle of the lithograph is preparing the dourra flour needed to make bread in accordance with a thousand-year-old method. Like all Europeans, Roberts was upset and revolted by the inhuman practice of slavery and, despite the bucolic appearance of this lithograph, he found the scene horrifying. Nearly all the slaves were frightened-looking young women and children; some appeared to be suffering from fever, and two, who lay at some distance from the others, seemed to be close to death. In Egypt, Abyssinian girls were quite expensive because of their good character, intelligence and great beauty.

The poor girls suffered greatly during the journey, but once purchased by their new masters were well fed and clothed, and treated kindly.

They usually joined the harems of the middle classes or a wealthy man. The merchants in the lithograph were handsome Nubians, apart from one brute with violent manners, certainly a drug addict, who for a while insisted on tormenting Roberts and his men in the vain attempt to conclude a deal. This lithograph, which represents invaluable evidence of an age that fortunately is no more, is of historical interest for a second reason. In the background, Roberts inserted a general view of the Temple of Amun at Wadi Dabod, actually several miles from Korti; the sanctuary was then practically intact, but a few decades later, around 1894, the first of the three pylons was swept away by the Nile.

**From David Roberts's journal:**

*November 14 - At Korti there are the remains of a very small temple which is hardly worth a visit. However, the town is quite interesting. On our arrival the inhabitants seemed very frightened, especially the women and children, who actually ran away. We were told that this strange behaviour is due to the fact that many of them are often carried away as slaves, and the mere appearance of a white man has the power to terrify them.*

# THE TEMPLE OF DAKKE

Plate 30

*November 14, 1838*

Two hours' march from Korti stood the magnificent ruins of the Temple of Dakke, a gem of architecture and sculpture that Roberts hastened to reach before sunset. The sanctuary, of moderate but very well balanced dimensions, was consecrated to the god Thoth of Pnubs, an Ethiopian town that the Greeks called Paotnuphis. The building which, unlike all the other Nubian temples, is oriented from north to south, was erected in the late 3rd century BC by order of Ethiopian King Arqamon and his contemporary, the Macedonian Pharaoh Ptolemy IV Philopator. Later, Ptolemy VII Evergete II added the pronaos, but the temple only acquired its final appearance during Roman rule, after the construction of the great pylon inserted in the outer boundary walls, which have almost disappeared.

Some reliefs and numerous inscriptions in Greek and Demotic by ancient visitors appear on the front façades of the two towers; the habit of leaving one's mark on monuments evidently dates back to a very early age. The colonnaded courtyard, which originally stood between the pylon and the pronaos, has been entirely destroyed, whereas the rear of the temple is well preserved.

The sanctuary of Dakke had to be dismantled after the construction of the Aswan High Dam and rebuilt at New Saboua; during the work it was discovered that some blocks, evidently reused, had belonged to an older temple dating from the age of Queen Hatshepsut and dedicated to the god Horus of Baki. That town, from which trails led to the gold mines of Umm Garayat, is now submerged under the waters of Lake Nasser.

Note the clearly incorrect date in the bottom right-hand corner of the lithograph, probably due to a mistake by Haghe or his assistants.

**From David Roberts's journal:**

*November 14 - The Temple of Dakke is of such exquisite workmanship that anyone wishing to take a perfect specimen of the beauty of Egyptian art back to Europe need travel no further.*

David Roberts, R.A. L. Haghe lith

DAKKE
in Nubia
Nov. 14th 1836

# THE ROCK TEMPLE OF GYRSHE

Plate 31

*November 15, 1838*

*R*oberts left Dakke in the late evening, and reached Gyrshe (which later became known as Gerf Hussein) in the middle of the night. Tireless as ever, at sunrise he was already on the way to the rise where a rock temple, excavated during the reign of Rameses II, stood. This lithograph and the description of the place in his travel journal now appear to be permeated by an aura of tragedy, for the sanctuary of "Rameses-Meryamun in the Dominion of Ptah" is lost for ever. The poor state of preservation of the structures, the crumbling rock, high costs and lack of time made it impracticable to save this monument during the UNESCO salvage campaign. Thus in the mid-sixties it fell victim to the waters of Lake Nasser together with countless burial grounds, rock tombs, votive shrines, chapels, and the ruins of fortresses, churches and Coptic monasteries.

The temple, consecrated to Ptah, Hathor, Ptah-Tatjenen and the deified Rameses II, was built by Setau, viceroy of Kush, the name by which Upper Nubia was then known; Lower Nubia was known as Wawat, while the Greeks called the whole region Ethiopia. A pronaos with columns built onto the rock wall preceded the hypogeal part, which was some 100 feet deep and consisted of the hypostyle room portrayed by Roberts, a transverse room and the cella containing the statues of the divinities.

The artist noted that the various rooms, inhabited by a myriad bats, had already deteriorated badly because of the fires lit by shepherds who had used the temple for shelter over the centuries. Many of the reliefs and hieroglyphics were by then indecipherable, but the hypostyle room, supported by six colossi portraying Rameses the Great with the headdress of Upper Egypt, maintained all of its mysterious fascination.

**From David Roberts's journal:**

*November 15 - We reached Gyrshe last night, and by daybreak this morning I was on my way to the hill where the temple is excavated. The ascent seems to have been originally a flight of steps, on each side of which the sphinxes now lying scattered about have been placed. Only two of the 12 columns of the portico are still standing, supporting a trabeation that projects from the living rock. There are various rooms, colossal statues and wall decorations in the temple, but all is badly damaged, and the figures on the walls are barely recognisable.*

Excavated Temple of Gyrshe - Nubia

D. Roberts

Temple of Kalabshee _ Nubia _ Nov.r 1838.

# THE TEMPLE OF KALABSHA

Plate 32

David Roberts, R.A. — L. Haghe, lith.

**From David Roberts's journal:**

*November 15 - After leaving Gyrshe, towards evening we were again in sight of the Temple of Kalabsha, the loveliest in Nubia. Situated in a loop of the river in the middle of a stretch of barren rocks, surrounded by palm and acacia trees, it is only seen to be ruined from close by. The reliefs have such clear-cut edges that they seem to have been recently carved, and the whole, with its elegant proportions and delicate details, is in no way inferior even to Philae.*

*November 15, 1838*

Satisfied by his visit to the Temple of Gyrshe, by the late afternoon on November 15, Roberts was already at Kalabsha, where he ordered the tents to be pitched for the night. As there was enough light and the sketches he had drawn on the outward journey were quite detailed, the artist had time to complete two views of the great sanctuary. The temple, considered the most grandiose Nubian monument after Abu Simbel, was built in the Ptolemaic period on the foundations of an older one, dating from the time of Amenhotep II and consecrated to the local god Mandulis, associated with Isis and Osiris. Rebuilt during the reign of Augustus, it remained almost entirely bare of decorations, and the little decoration there appears unfinished.
The 245-foot-long building could be reached from the Nile along a processional route that climbed to two huge platforms built at different levels, both in front of the pylon. The façade of the pylon has no reliefs, and its plainness is only relieved by the usual grooves in which the flagpoles of the sacred banners were fixed. The impressive size of the temple was justified by the strategic importance of Talmis, the ancient name of Kalabsha, which stood guard over a narrow stretch of the Nile; the building was converted into a church and fell into ruin after the Arab conquest.
In the lithograph, humble mud dwellings seem to huddle around the massive bulk of the temple, and even cluster on the roof of the naos, as if seeking protection, to form a scenario common to nearly all the Egyptian archaeological sites in the 19th century. The place drawn by Roberts no longer exists today, as it was submerged by the waters of Lake Nasser; all that survives is the temple, which, between 1961 and 1963, was dismantled and rebuilt 25 miles further south at New Kalabsha, at the western end of the Great Aswan Dam.

# THE PRONAOS OF THE TEMPLE OF KALABSHA

Plate 33

*November 15, 1838*

**B**eyond the pylon is a courtyard surrounded on three sides by a portico, most of whose columns had fallen and been buried by debris when Roberts saw them. The end wall is constituted by the façade of the atrium, in the middle of which is an impressive portal. According to the canons of Egyptian Ptolemaic and Roman art, the intercolumniations are partly closed by screens covered with bas-reliefs portraying, among other things, the gods Thot and Horus performing libations by pouring holy water onto the sovereign. On one of the columns, a long inscription in Meroitic (the language spoken by the Nubians under Ptolemaic and Roman rule) recounts the victory of King Silko over his eternal enemies the Blemmyes; the epigraph is translated into bad Greek on one of the intercolumnar walls. In the atrium, 12 columns with capitals featuring plant designs support the ceiling, much of which has now collapsed. Of the various reliefs present here, two are of some interest; the first shows one of the Ptolemies making offerings to Mandulis, while the other portrays the founder of the first sanctuary, Amenhotep II, offering wine to Min and the patron god of the temple. The atrium is followed by the sacrarium, formed by three successive chambers that leave enough space around

them for a corridor inside the perimeter wall, built as a continuance of the side walls of the courtyard. The complex was enclosed by a high embankment that formed a corridor similar to the previous one. This plan simplifies the elements of the typical Ptolemaic-Roman temple, while still retaining its general layout.

Temple at Tafa in
Nubia
Nov. 18th 183...

# THE RUINS OF THE TEMPLE OF TAFA

Plate 34

*November 16, 1838*

*F*rom Abu Simbel onwards the Scotsman ordered his men to stop frequently, not only so that he could draw the ruined monuments in the various places but also to enable him to buy ancient coins, swords, amulets and small antiques, or to ask the most attractive girls to pose for him. These breaks were welcomed by his men, who were becoming increasingly lazy as a result of women's company and banquets. In the preceding few days he had often had to resort to threats and flattery to make them row faster, but whenever he became engrossed in sketching his supervision ceased, and the crew returned on board even less eagerly than before. The same thing happened at Kalabsha, and Roberts had a certain amount of trouble persuading the crew to depart for Tafa, where he arrived on the morning of November 16. Here, not far from Wadi Kardassy, stood two small temples very similar to others he had already seen in the region. It is fortunate that Roberts decided to draw this, the most badly damaged one; while the north temple, which was almost intact, was donated to the Netherlands and has been on display at the National Museum in Leyden since 1978, the south temple was used as a source of reusable materials from 1870 onwards, and was entirely dismantled.

The sanctuary, which together with its neighbor formed the religious center of the Roman settlement of Taphis, was founded in the late Ptolemaic period and extensively rebuilt during the Roman occupation of Lower Nubia. Roberts described it as a building of rather modest manufacture and unharmonious proportions, surrounded by architectural fragments scattered over the adjacent plain.

# THE LITTLE TEMPLE OF WADI KARDASSY

Plate 35

*November 16, 1838*

As the day was not too hot, Roberts continued on foot from Tafa to Wadi Kardassy. On his way he passed through various villages, whose inhabitants crowded around him curiously. In the early afternoon he finally came in sight of the rocky plateau on which stood a small kiosk, consecrated to the goddess Isis, that was similar in layout to the one on Philae. At that time the building, which overlooked the Nile, constituted one of the most impressive scenes in all of Lower Nubia. Sadly, following the construction of the Sadd el-Ali (High Dam) at Aswan, this site disappeared, engulfed by the huge mass of water of the reservoir, which, with an area of 2,100 square miles and a length of 316 miles, is the second largest in the world. Lake Nasser has brought undeniable financial advantages to Egypt, but at the same time has upset the ecological balance in the region and inflicted untold damage on the archaeological heritage and landscape of Nubia.

Temple of Wady Kardasoy
Nubia

Ruins of the Temple of Kardaseh, Nubia.

# THE LITTLE TEMPLE OF WADI KARDASSY WITH THE NILE IN THE BACKGROUND

Plate 36

*November 16, 1838*

*David Roberts R.A.*

The little temple, or rather the kiosk, of Kardassy is a small building only about ten square yards, built in the late Ptolemaic period and completed during Roman rule. It was originally formed by ten columns connected by low intercolumnar walls, only six of which are still standing; the two on either side of the portal are surmounted by elegant capitals with the face of the goddess Hathor, while the others support capitals of floral inspiration.

It is interesting to note that the two Hathor capitals in turn support two stylized altars, containing an asp.

As can be clearly seen in the lithograph, this building, unlike the Temple of Philae, which was never finished, was roofed with huge monolithic slabs, all but one of which have been destroyed. The intercolumnar walls are bare, apart from the long row of uraei surrounding the upper strip and the winged solar disks appearing immediately below it.

As demonstrated by a number of crosses carved inside it, the building was used as a church until the advent of Islam. The Roman legionnaires built a fortress near the temple to guard traffic along the Nile and the nearby stone quarries. The kiosk of Kardassy was dismantled during the campaign to save the Nubian temples and reassembled near the Temple of Kalabsha, some 25 miles away from its ancient site. Unfortunately, its new location is far less spectacular than the original one.

**From David Roberts's journal:**

*November 16 - It is hard to guess at the age of the building from its condition, as the devastation which has spoilt it seems to have been wreaked but yesterday. The temple is dazzling in the sunlight against the deep blue of the sky, and it almost seems as though the hand of its destroyers had just ceased its work. Because of the total absence of moisture, the stones ring like bells at the slightest touch.*

# A GROUP OF NUBIANS NEAR THE TEMPLE OF WADI KARDASSY

Plate 37

*November 16, 1838*

*A*t Wadi Kardassy, Roberts bought some copper coins from a woman, while a man offered him a long sword (which he described as being similar to those carried by the Scottish Highlanders) and another smaller one that he wore hanging from his belt. Keen to strike a bargain like all self-respecting tourists, Roberts also bought from the same man an attractive bracelet that he saw on his left arm, a small hippopotamus-hide shield and a water bottle with a hide cover decorated with shells, all for only 30 shillings, which was a very reasonable price even for that period.

*Especially at first, Roberts had no great respect for the Nubians, who to his Western eyes seemed little more than savages. Only long acquaintance with the two Nubians in the crew, both called Hassan, and the slowly dawning realization of how much those people suffered from harassment* by slave traders and compulsory conscription by Pasha Mohammed Ali, led him to mitigate his opinion considerably. Above all, he truly admired the physical appearance and sincere friendliness of the Nubians, "with their well-proportioned bodies and frank, intelligent expressions." However, he was appalled by the women's habit of smearing themselves with butter or castor oil to soften their skin and keep away parasites, mainly because of the nauseous smell that ceaselessly issued from their bodies; otherwise, he considered them splendid, indeed desirable. Far less prejudiced than he had been only a few days earlier, at Wadi Kardassy Roberts decided to immortalize a group of local inhabitants, many of whom wore a singular hairstyle of very ancient origin. Of the weapons they held, only the spears were part of their usual equipment; they had brought the long swords and shields to sell.

David Roberts, R.A. — L. Haghe, Lith.

# THE NILE NEAR WADI DABOD

Plate 38

*November 16, 1838*

R oberts left Wadi Kardassy in the afternoon, and came in sight of the heights of Wadi Dabod at sunset. As the boat sailed along, following the placid current of the river, his attention was attracted by a number of crocodiles basking on the sandy shores, as if to absorb the last rays of the sun. These formidable reptiles, up to 20 feet long, with an array of lethal teeth, were the true rulers of the Nile for centuries, feared and respected by the local people to the extent of being worshipped as the earthly manifestation of a deity, Sobek of Kom Ombo. The cult of this god had some interesting features. In various regions the crocodile was worshipped in ancient times as the supreme deity, but later began to be identified first as an ally and then as the actual personification of Set, the god of evil and enemy of Osiris, so that the crocodile itself became less and less important. However, the danger represented by the great predator was still sufficient to win it the terrified respect of those who had to cross the river every day; its sly movements, exceptional strength and speed made it a formidable enemy.

There were numerous crocodiles between Gebel el-Silsila and Kom Ombo; they lived in large family groups on the sandbanks and in the shallows in the middle of the river, taking a heavy toll of human lives every year. It is therefore easy to understand why Sobek continued to be worshipped with particular fervor in the region, and his image was frequently evoked as a propitiatory totem by boatmen. Even in the 19th century, blood-curdling tales were told about crocodiles, and the local people were terrified of them. They only lost their supremacy on the river after the construction of the first Aswan Dam, and they have now almost disappeared from the part of the Nile that flows through Egypt. Although the lithograph is very effective, it is highly unlikely that the artist ventured very close to the lethal creatures; he probably left this doubtful privilege to the herons shown in the plate, who earned their safety and food by picking parasites off these descendants of the prehistoric dinosaurs.

# GENERAL VIEW
# OF THE ISLAND OF PHILAE

Plate 39

*November 17–18, 1838*

On November 17, when darkness fell, Roberts was back on the Island of Philae, where he spent the next two days drawing the temples that had so impressed him less than three weeks earlier. This stop was welcomed with great enthusiasm by Hassan Amoris (so called to distinguish him from a fellow crew member also called Hassan), as the beautiful wife who had won him his nickname lived in the region of the First Cataract. This magnificent view shows the entire complex, seen from the heights of the nearby of different periods, although most of the buildings date from the Ptolemaic-Roman period. On the far right of the lithograph is the Kiosk of Nectanebo and the neighboring obelisk, both dating from the 4th century BC; opposite them are the two wings of the colonnade built by Augustus. Next to the first pylon is the portal of Ptolemy II, evidently surviving from an older building; in the background is the great Kiosk of Trajan. Between the two pylons is a large courtyard: the side overlooking the river is

island of Biggé. The temple, consecrated to the goddess Isis and her son Harpocrates, a local form of the god Horus, stands on the site of an older sanctuary, probably built by Nectanebo, the first pharaoh for whom dated remains have been found on the site. The complex presents a succession of heterogeneous elements closed by a mammisi, whose rear façade can be seen here. On the wharf opposite it, overlooking the Nile, stands the great portal of Hadrian. The Temple of Isis proper, consisting of an atrium and the naos, surrounded by some secondary rooms, stands behind the second pylon.

Ruins Temple on the Island of Berigh Nubia

# THE RUINS OF A LITTLE TEMPLE ON THE ISLE OF BIGGÉ

Plate 40

*November 18, 1838*

*In ancient times, no one but the priests of nearby Philae could set foot on the Isle of Biggé, sacred to Hathor and Ups, the goddess of fire; this was the site of the famous Abaton, the tomb of Osiris. The sepulchre, whose name roughly signifies "pure mound," lay in the middle of a wood; all around were 365 small altars, and milk was poured onto one of them every day in rotation as a libation to the god. The vital spirit of Osiris, in the form of a bird, was thus able to feed daily. Every ten days, the effigy of Isis was carried to the island on a sacred boat from the nearby sanctuary of Philae so that the goddess could visit her consort. Once a year,*

*on the occasion of a solemn festival, Isis was accompanied on her pilgrimage by her son Harendotes, "Horus who defends the father." A sanctuary was built during the 18th dynasty at Biggé, where total silence was observed so as not to disturb the sleep of the god, and then rebuilt around 245 BC by Ptolemy III Evergete. This building was further extended by Ptolemy XIII, who also built a large entrance portal. An arch, later added to this portal, led from the wharf on the Nile to the sanctuary via a staircase. A comparison of Roberts's lithograph with the photo of the same site shows the extent to which the waters of the Nile rose after the construction of the High Dam.*

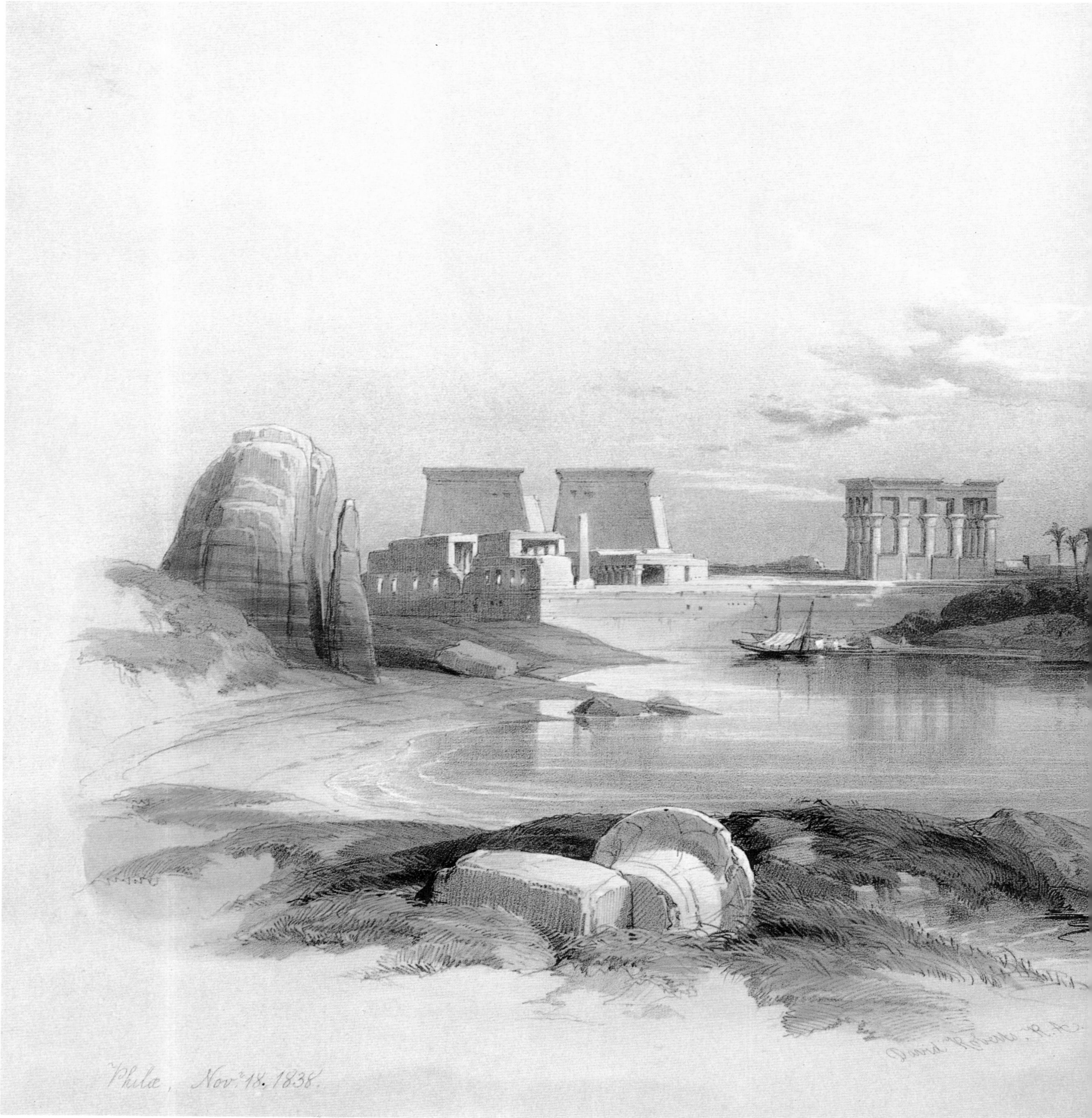
Philæ, Novr. 18. 1838.

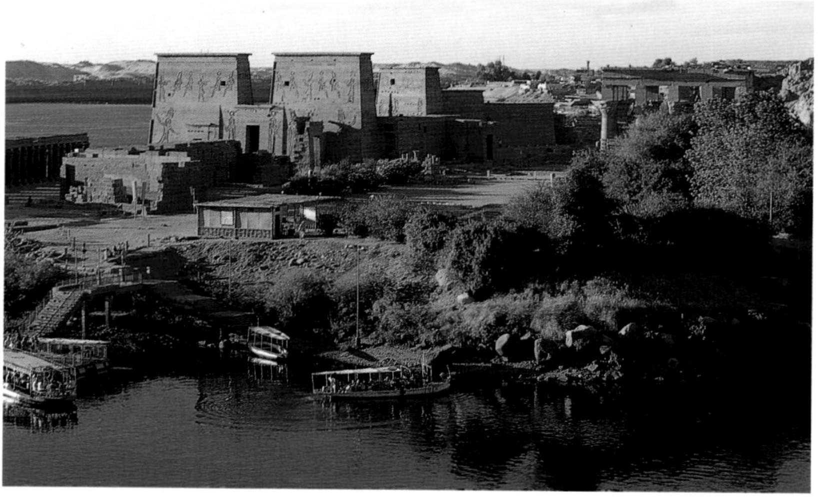

# THE TEMPLES OF PHILAE SEEN FROM THE SOUTH

Plate 41

*November 18, 1838*

From whatever angle he observed it, Roberts was enchanted by the magnificent sight of the sanctuary of Philae, which must have filled the pilgrims drawn to the spot by the esoteric popularity of Isis with even more reverential admiration. That divinity, daughter of the sun god Ra and wife and sister of Osiris, held a privileged position in the Egyptian pantheon as she was an expert in mysteries and powerful spells. She used her magic arts thaumaturgically on her divine husband after his treacherous brother Set, god of chaos, cut his body to pieces. Isis was considered the protectress of the dead, and at the same time was represented as the creating mother goddess in the region of the cataracts; when a Nubian dynasty settled in Thebes in the 7th century BC, her worship became more widely known, and eventually spread beyond the borders of Egypt. The cult of Isis became particularly popular in the Ptolemaic and Roman period, when the sanctuary of Philae reached the heights of its glory; the sick and lame flocked there from all parts of the country and the various provinces of the Empire, trusting in the favors of the goddess. The Christian repression was proportional to the fame gained by Isis; the followers of the new religion attacked the reliefs decorating the temple, which was transformed into a church, with blind fury. However, the petitions and prayers carved in numerous parts of the sanctuary demonstrate that the island was still for some time the last stronghold in Egypt of the thousand-year-old religious tradition.

# THE GREAT COLONNADE IN FRONT OF THE TEMPLE OF ISIS ON PHILAE

Plate 42

*November 19, 1838*

The pilgrims who flocked to the sanctuary, like modern visitors, disembarked at the southernmost tip of the island, where they were welcomed to the "kiosk of Nectanebo" not by Isis but another goddess, the benevolent cow-eared Hathor. The effigy of the mysterious goddess of beauty and pleasure appears above the capitals of six columns, the only ones left out of the 14 that were part of the restoration work on the building ordered by Ptolemy II Philadelphus; the two sovereigns are immortalized in the reliefs on the intercolumnar walls as they present their offerings to the gods. Beyond the pavilion stands the great colonnade, of exceptional scenic effect. The west side, parallel to the coastline, stretches for some 330 feet, with a row of 32 columns supporting capitals with complex shapes inspired by the plant kingdom. Stars and vultures are portrayed on the ceiling, which represents the sky. The reliefs decorating the end wall portray Octavian and Nero, whose stylized features were intended to emphasize the divine origin of the new sovereigns of Egypt. On the columns, the Emperor Tiberius brings his own offerings to the local divinities. The east colonnade on the opposite side of the courtyard was never completed; some of the 17 columns are bare of decoration, and 11 are surmounted by unfinished capitals. A third of the way along the flat area near the longer side, an underground staircase leads to the Nilometer. Nearly every temple in Egypt had a well of this kind with a gauge on the wall so that the river level could be read. Knowledge of the pattern of floods of the Nile was of great economic and social importance, as it enabled the size of the harvest and consequently the amount of the taxes to be forecasted. Only the priests held the privilege of announcing the readings of the Nilometer. The complex perspective design, admirably reproduced by Roberts, concludes at the end with the great pylon of the Temple of Isis, 60 feet tall and 150 feet wide. Begun by Ptolemy II, it was completed by his successor Ptolemy III, but the decoration work continued in subsequent eras. On the two towers Ptolemy XII Neos Dionysus is portrayed as he offers the submission of his prisoners to Isis; on the upper parts the pharaoh is received by Isis, who is accompanied by her son Horus and sister Neftis. The winged solar disk appears above the portal.

*Grand Approach to the Temple of Philae. Nubia.*

# THE INTERIOR OF THE TEMPLE OF ISIS ON PHILAE

<u>Plate 43</u>

*November 19, 1838*

*D*uring his first visit, Roberts had marveled at the exquisite proportions and magnificent bas-reliefs of the interior of the temple. He also found the paintings to be in an exceptional state of preservation. In his journal, the entry for October 30 states, "I was entranced by the splendid composition of its colours; they seem to be freshly painted, and even in the places where they are most exposed to the implacable sunlight, they have retained their radiant freshness." We are fortunate that the artist decided to spend November 19 drawing the interior of the sanctuary, because the long period spent in the waters of the reservoir has almost wiped out all traces of these elegant colors. Roberts's illustration shows the hypostyle room of the temple proper, situated immediately after the second pylon, which is smaller than the first. This room, in which eight columns support the ceiling, is preceded by an unroofed courtyard, along the shorter sides of which run two short porticoes, each supported by a central column, which constitute two extensions to the hypostyle room. That room is followed by some vestibules and the naos, surrounded by various minor rooms. The initial sequence of these rooms can be seen in the lithograph. The walls and columns are covered with inscriptions and reliefs that show the pharaohs of the Ptolemaic dynasty and the Roman emperors Augustus, Tiberius and Antoninus Pius making offerings to Isis or performing religious rites. The courtyard could be covered with a velarium (canopy) operated by ropes; the holes through which the ropes ran can still be seen in the molding facing the pylon.

**From David Roberts's journal:**

*November 19 - Today I made some drawings of the interior of the temple and copied many of the figures covering the walls, all in excellent condition, with brilliant colours.*

Grand Portico of the Temple of Philæ. Nubia.

# THE HYPOSTYLE ROOM IN THE
# TEMPLE OF ISIS ON PHILAE

Plate 44

*November 19, 1838*

*T*his lithograph repeats the same subject as the previous one, but from a different angle. The hypostyle room was originally separated from the small inner courtyard by the usual intercolumnar walls, typical of the sacred architecture of the Ptolemaic period, which framed a central portal. This is one of the most attractive of all the lithographs because of its very effective composition and the meticulous care lavished on the decorative details. Pharaohs and divinities repeat their hieratic gestures endlessly, while the great columns almost seem to blossom into the glorious array of shapes and colors in the capitals, which, apparently effortlessly, support the mighty trabeations along which sacred ships sail. The figures of great vultures with outspread wings, repeated in long rows, stand out on the ceilings, painted like starry skies. Some Coptic crosses carved on the shaft of the columns and the remains of an altar, which demonstrate the conversion of the temple into a Christian church, can be clearly seen in the illustration. As an inscription explains, this "good work" was performed under Bishop Theodore, at the time of the Emperor

Justinian and Empress Theodora in the 6th century. Another inscription still visible today commemorates the "archaeological expedition" sent here by Pope Gregory XVI in 1841. Sadly, this interference inflicted great damage on the magnificent sanctuary, although its charm still remains intact, just as it was at the height of Isis' glory.

# The Island of Philae
## AT SUNSET

Plate 45

*November 19, 1838*

*An interesting feature of Roberts's lithographs is that they show the age-old appearance of the Island of Philae and its monuments, which remained unchanged until the construction of the First Aswan Dam. The dam brought undeniable financial advantages to Egypt, but also meant the beginning of a terrible ordeal for its monuments. Already half-flooded by the waters of the new reservoir, the temple suffered a far worse affront in 1934, when the dam was raised by several feet, causing the almost total flooding of the complex.*

*Its agony was only alleviated for three months a year, sometime between August and December, when the crest gates were raised, revealing the mud-covered structures as in an apparition. The soil of what was once the "garden island" then reawoke, producing lush vegetation to welcome the rare visitors to the dying archaeological site. It seemed that the destiny of Philae was to become even more tragic when the mammoth task of building the High Dam began in 1960. The monuments that had resisted only thanks to the strengthening of the foundations could not have borne the daily variations in the water level. Fortunately, during*

*the campaign to save the Nubian monuments promoted by the United Nations, the drastic decision to move the sanctuary of the goddess Isis was taken. The choice of the new site fell on the higher nearby island of Agilkia, but considerable extension work was needed to orient the monuments correctly. The dismantling and reconstruction of all the architectural structures was put out to international tender in 1969, and the successful bidder was an Italian company. Work began in 1972, when pile-driving boats began to drive 3,000 steel piles into the bottom of the reservoir. These piles enclosed the island in two concentric dams that were to form the base of a mighty ring-shaped dam. The water was than pumped out and the mud removed by hundreds of workmen. In the meantime, the ground was leveled at Agilkia by 100 feet, and the coastline was extended.*

*On September 9, 1975, the first of the 37,363 blocks of the complex were removed, and reassembly work began on the nearby island on May 29, 1977. Three years later, on March 10, New Philae was inaugurated. The only remaining sign of the long decades during which the complex was underwater is the grayish color of the lower parts of the structures.*

Kom Ombo
Nov. 21st 1838.

**From David Roberts's journal:**

*November 21 - I made two drawings of these magnificent ruins, and at sunset I painted a complete view of the place in oils.*

David Roberts, R.A. — L. Haghe, lith.

# THE TEMPLE OF KOM OMBO

Plate 46

*November 20–21, 1838*

*A*t daybreak on November 20, the crew began the complex maneuvers required for the dangerous descent of the First Cataract, which had created considerable problems on the outward journey. Towards evening the boat had finally come through the rapids safe and sound, but the captain was understandably exhausted. Until the first dam was built across the Nile between 1898 and 1912 and an annexed canal was constructed to allow even barges of very high tonnage to pass, the only way of crossing the cataract was for the boats to be harnessed and hauled across by men and animals; the effort required was enormous, and accidents were commonplace. After spending the night at Aswan, the next day Roberts and his men came in sight of the ruins of Kom Ombo, where they pitched their tents. Now a flourishing agricultural town on the right bank of the Nile, before the 4th century BC Kom Ombo was a powerful stronghold erected to defend the lower reaches of the Nile. Although no monumental ruins prior to the 18th dynasty survive, it is known that a fairly important sanctuary must have stood there during the Middle Kingdom (2100–1750 BC), and that it was later extended by Rameses II.

The area only acquired great political and religious importance under the reign of the Ptolemies, when it became the capital of a nome (province) and the construction of the second temple, whose remains are still visible, was commenced. Work began during the reign of Ptolemy V, around 204 BC, and continued for some 90 years, but the wall structures were not finished until the time of Ptolemy XIII Neos Dionysus, one century and a half after the foundation. The porticoed courtyard was completed by Roman Emperor Tiberius, and some other additions and decorations were ordered by Domitian towards the end of the 1st century AD. However, inscriptions bearing the names of the emperors Geta, Caracalla and Macrinus have also been found, and the bas-reliefs referring to the latter are the latest to survive from pagan Egypt.
The word kom means "hill" in Arabic, and in fact the temple (very unusually for this region) stands on a kind of low acropolis overlooking a large loop of the river. The position of the site, which was subject to continual erosion by the river, caused the ruin of much of the complex, now protected by a large embankment.

# THE RUINS OF THE TEMPLE OF KOM OMBO

Plate 47

*November 21, 1838*

When Roberts visited the ruins of Kom Ombo, much of the sanctuary was still buried under the sand. Systematic excavation work did not begin until 1893, revealing the most unusual detail of the building, namely that it was a double temple, the only one of its kind in Egypt. Nearly all the Egyptian sanctuaries were consecrated to more than one god, as in the case of Karnak, where the Theban Triad was worshipped, but the effigy of the main deity usually occupied the central naos, while those of the secondary deities were placed in the side chapels.

Only at Kom Ombo was the building divided into two parts, separated by an imaginary longitudinal line; the right-hand part was dedicated to Sobek, associated in the triad with Hathor and Khonsu, and the left-hand part to Horus, accompanied by Senetnofret and Penebtaui. The structure thus consisted of two identical adjacent sectors, each of which was independent of the other for the purpose of worship. There were two entrances in the pylon and the same number in the pronaos, the hypostyle room and the chambers preceding the two cellae. The building did not appear to be formed by two separate, adjacent temples, because there were no tangible internal boundaries except in the naos. Equally, the unusual duality of Kom Ombo never gave it the appearance of a twinship, still less of inviting competition between the two deities. The design of the temple was in fact due to the policy of the Ptolemies who, wishing to confirm their sovereignty over Upper and Lower Egypt, were first crowned in Alexandria, and then crowned again at Kom Ombo. To emphasize and at the same time sanction this double supremacy, the temple was consecrated to Haroeris, traditional patron of the pharaohs who unified the country, and to the crocodile-headed Sobek, worshipped and feared since time immemorial by the inhabitants of Nubia. In Roberts's time, and until the construction of the First Dam, the great reptile was a very common and disquieting sight along the banks of the river.

Kom Ombo.
Nov 21st 1838

# THE NILE IN THE VICINITY OF GEBEL SILSILA

Plate 48

*November 22, 1838*

*After leaving behind the glorious ruins of Kom Ombo on the evening of November 21, Roberts and his men spent the whole night on board, sailing north. What they saw the next day at dawn near Gebel Silsila surprised them: a steep ridge also known as the Chain Mountains. Here the Nile forms a gorge in which the waters become ever more restless until they form rapids and whirlpools, which, in ancient times gained it the name of Khenu, "The place where you have to row." Not far from the point where the river narrows, the ancient sandstone quarries, which were exploited during the New Kingdom to build the Ramesseum, can still be seen on the east bank.*
*All around stand the remains of the town of Kheni and the village where the quarrymen lived with their families, together with some commemorative rock inscriptions bearing the names of Amenhotep IV and Seti I.*

*However, the most important monuments are situated on the west bank, where votive shrines and inscriptions are far more numerous. The most interesting monument is the great rock chapel of Horemheb, covered with decorations. Though his curiosity was aroused by the singular shapes of the surrounding rocks, probably due to ancient mining activity, Roberts decided not to stop, partly so as not to overtire the oarsmen who had found the right pace.*
*He therefore merely completed the drawing he had begun on the outward journey, and spent the rest of the day spreading fixative on the finished works.*
*A shaduf, one of the numerous lever-operated wells with which Egyptian peasants drew water from the Nile for irrigation purposes, is shown in the foreground of the lithograph. This ancient device, consisting of a long arm to which a bucket and a counterweight are fixed, is still in common use today.*

# THE TEMPLE OF EDFU

Plate 49

*November 22, 1838*

On the evening of the 22nd Roberts reached Edfu, whose temple seemed to him even more beautiful than anything he had seen so far. At sunset the sun flooded the sanctuary with a particularly warm light, and he had all the time he needed to draw a general view of the building. As he had noted on the outward journey, the building, though impressive, was not excessively large and appeared well proportioned from every point of view; the pylon in particular was a masterpiece of balance and architectural elegance.

The temple, which was excavated and restored in 1860 by French archaeologist Auguste Mariette, was consecrated to "Horus of the variegated feathers," the patron god of the district, represented alternatively in the form of a hawk, a person with a hawk's head or a winged solar disk. Despite Roberts's comments, Edfu, which is 450 feet long, 260 feet wide and 86 feet high at the top of the portal, is the largest religious complex in Egypt apart from the great temple of Amun at Karnak. It is also the least damaged. The perfect state of preservation of this huge monument means that it provides a great deal

of information about the architectural organization of the other Egyptian temples, often ruined or incomplete because of collapses and destruction. Begun in 237 BC by Ptolemy III Evergete and concluded 180 years later by Ptolemy XIII, the temple follows the distribution pattern developed towards the end of the New Kingdom, with a further addition of antechambers and stricter distribution of the interior space, especially around the saccellum. The sanctuary is entered through the great portal, which, flanked by two massive trapezoidal towers, forms the pylon. It is still impressive, although even when Roberts drew the temple it lacked the great molding that once crowned the summit. Its present height is nearly 124 feet.
The pylon is followed by the great porticoed courtyard enclosed by 32 columns and overlooked by the hypostyle pronaos. This huge room leads to what is known as the "banqueting hall," a second pronaos whose ceiling is also supported by columns.
Finally, two successive vestibules lead to the naos, the actual sacrarium, around which ten chapels consecrated to minor divinities are distributed.

David Roberts R.A.

David Roberts R. A. Litho(?) by

Portico of The Temple Edfou Upper Egypt Novr 25th 1838

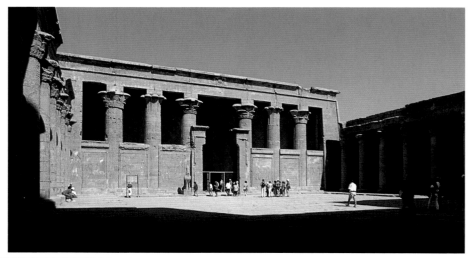

# THE PRONAOS OF THE TEMPLE OF EDFU

Plate 50

*November 23, 1838*

Roberts was fascinated by the perfect proportions of the Temple of Edfu, and by the magnificent polychrome bas-reliefs that decorated every surface. Braving the unbearable heat, the day after his arrival he drew two views of the superb colonnaded courtyard, the sight of which irresistibly attracted him. In fact, the sanctuary of Edfu almost gives the impression that Egypt itself, as it began its slow decline after the most glorious period of its history, wished to demonstrate its artistic skills for the very last time. In 30 BC, only 27 years after the work was finished, Augustus suppressed the last vestiges of the power of the Ptolemies, and brought Egypt firmly under the Roman yoke.

The Caesars were also fascinated by the majesty of the sanctuary, however, and took steps to ensure that it did not fall into ruin.

The pronaos, with six columns facing onto the great courtyard, is perhaps the most spectacular part of the temple. It clearly demonstrates the preference of Ptolemaic taste for capitals of highly complex forms, quite different from the classical designs; the two nearest to the portal are shaped like lotus flowers, the ones in the middle are decorated with date-palm leaves, and the outer ones are inspired by the fronds of Hyphaene thebaica, *a palm tree typical of the region. Inside, 12 more columns arranged in pairs support the ceiling; here again, the capitals present a very wide variety of shapes.*

**From David Roberts's journal:**

*November 23 - Today I made two large drawings, one of the pronaos and one from under it, towards the pylon. To draw the former I was obliged to sit in the sun protected only by a sunshade, and the temperature reached 98°F in the shade today. I fear I did not make a very good job of it, but this colonnade is so lovely I could not resist it. From now on I will avoid exposing myself excessively to the sun, although by so doing I risk missing some interesting subjects.*

# THE PYLON OF THE TEMPLE OF EDFU SEEN FROM THE PRONAOS

Plate 51

*November 23, 1838*

When looking at lithographs like this one, it should not be forgotten that before taking up painting Roberts was a talented decorator, and had painted sets for the most famous theaters in Scotland for many years. The pronaos and the great colonnaded courtyard of the sanctuary of Edfu, with their admirable perspective and the rigid symmetry of the architectural modules tempered by a profusion of ornamental elements, could not fail to galvanize Roberts's attention. This explains his evident, repeated preference for the same subject, interpreted from three different angles. From the standpoint of composition, this plate is probably one of the most successful in the entire collection; the bold insertion of the architrave in the foreground achieves the result of expanding the exterior space to the full, while the clever play of chiaroscuro suggests an almost instinctive perception of the contrast between the burning sand flooded by sunlight and the coolness offered by the shade.

The great bas-reliefs that decorate the inner walls of the pylon (perfectly reproduced by Roberts) show Ptolemy XIII Neos Dionysus making offerings to the local divinities Horus, Hathor and their son Ihy. The winged solar disk, symbol of the patron god of Edfu, is clearly visible on the jamb of the portal; a polychrome version of this symbol also appears on the architrave of the pronaos. The great courtyard, to which the faithful flocked on feast days, is surrounded by a portico whose columns end in elaborate capitals of floral inspiration. At the sight of such magnificence, Roberts greatly regretted that the interior of the temple was wholly inaccessible.

from under the Portico of Temple of Edfu—Upper Egypt

# The Façade of the Pronaos in the Temple of Edfu

Plate 52

*November 24, 1838*

During his first visit to Edfu on October 26, Roberts had described the temple as the loveliest in Egypt, so well proportioned in every part that it appeared perfect from every point of view. With a taste wholly in keeping with the romanticism of his age, he added that the fact that it was half-buried in the sand made it look even more delightful, as it reminded him of the views of the Roman forums drawn by Piranesi.

This time the artist drew the façade of the pronaos from the southeast, focusing all his attention on the huge capitals that surmount the columns and on the complex hieroglyphics that cover nearly all the available space. Unfortunately, because of the sand that obstructed much of the building, the Scottish artist was unable to see the wall built to halfway up the lateral intercolumniations, which has no openings except at the portal in the center, another element typical of Ptolemaic architecture.

Much interested in the details of local life, Roberts painted a portrait of a weaver at work under the portico in the background. As in the three previous illustrations, some of the miserable wattle and daub huts that had sprung up like birds' nests all over the building, ruining its magnificent proportions, can be seen above the huge trabeation of the pronaos. These hovels were later demolished by Mariette.

Unusually, this lithograph is correctly dated – almost a tangible sign of the vivid impression that the Temple of Edfu left in Roberts's memory.

David Roberts. R.A.—L. Haghe lith.

**From David Roberts's journal:**

*November 24 - Today the thermometer read over 98°F in the shade, and even with the aid of a sunshade and a tent, drawing was extremely tiring.*

# THE INTERIOR OF THE TEMPLE OF ESNA

Plate 53

*November 25, 1838*

Incessantly urged on by Hassan Amoris, the crew spent the whole night manning the oars, and as day broke the boat reached Esna, 30 miles north of Edfu. Although the remains of the temple of Knhum could not bear comparison with the size of the splendid sanctuary he had visited in the past few days, Roberts did not have the heart to pass it by without drawing it; its decorations were in no way inferior to those of any other temple in terms of quality and wealth of details. In fact, the monument remains to this day the greatest pride of this ancient city, whose economy is still largely based on trade in high-quality fabrics and the camel market. The sovereigns of the 18th dynasty, who governed the country around 1500 BC, built the first temple dedicated to the ram's-head god, considered by the local people to be the creator of the human race, who modeled on his potter's wheel the egg that generated every form of life. Under the rule of the Saites the temple was partly renovated, but it was not until AD 181 that Ptolemy VI Philometor began total reconstruction work. The sanctuary was later extended under Roman rule. The building, which may have been surrounded by an outer wall, consisted of the pronaos or hypostyle room, two vestibules, the cella, and two antechambers connected by corridors. The hypostyle room is the only structure that has survived intact through the centuries. The façade, with six columns whose intercolumniations are occupied by partition walls built to halfway up, fully reflects the Ptolemaic building styles, whereas the main body of the building was completed in the second half of the 1st century AD during the rule of the emperors Tiberius, Claudius and Vespasian. The latter is described in a dedicatory inscription as "the lord of capital Rome." The uniqueness of the Temple of Esna lies in the fact that it is entirely covered with reliefs. The walls and columns are decorated with religious texts covering an unusual variety of subjects; they recount the origin of the world, life and its transmission, the creation of man and the theological bases of royal power. The most important parts were carved during the reigns of Trajan and Hadrian (2nd century AD), while the most recent are attributed to Decius (AD 250), and constitute the last known collection of hieroglyphic inscriptions. The ceiling of the hypostyle room, supported by 18 columns whose capitals are finely carved with nature motifs, is decorated with some splendid astronomical scenes.

Because of the accumulation of debris all around it, the temple now lies 30 feet below road level. When Roberts visited the site it was accessible by climbing down a ladder. At that time the room was used as a powder magazine; it was later converted into a corn and cotton store for a few years.

**From David Roberts's journal:**

*November 25 - While I was at work,
I was surrounded by a group of very
friendly Coptic Christians, who seemed
to consider me as one of them.
I portrayed some of them in my
drawing, which they very much
enjoyed. Esna is the last Christian
town on the Nile before Abyssinia.
When I went back on board, I found
Hassan Amoris suffering from terrible
pains; thinking that he had cholera,
I administered 30 drops of laudanum.
To my great relief, he recovered in a few
hours.*

# THE RUINS OF THE TEMPLE OF HERMONTHIS

Plate 54

*November 26, 1838*

When Hassan Amoris recovered from a bout of fever that caused serious concern to Roberts and the crew for some hours, the boat set sail from Esna, reaching Erment during the night.

The Scotsman went ashore in the early morning and spent several hours drawing the temple of Montu, which he had considered very picturesque on the outward journey.

The town, situated around 12 miles from Luxor, was probably the birthplace of the sovereigns of the 11th dynasty, who founded the important sanctuary there; known by the name of Iuni, it was also called Per-Montu (Dominion of Montu) because the hawk-headed god of war was worshipped there. In the Roman period, when it was known by the Greek name of Hermonthis,

it became the capital of a fairly flourishing nome. The temple, which was rebuilt first by order of Nectanebo II and later by two sovereigns of the Ptolemy dynasty, Cleopatra VII and Ptolemy XV Caesarion, remained open for worship during Roman rule.

This plate is of great historical and archaeological value because the building, which was already very dilapidated and partly occupied by the sheik's residence when Roberts saw it, was razed to the ground a few years after Roberts's visit so that its stones could be used to build a great sugar refinery and wharves on the Nile.

During excavations conducted on several occasions this century, the necropolises where the bulls consecrated to Montu and the cows that gave birth to them were buried were uncovered a few miles north of the town.

# VIEW OF THE TEMPLES OF KARNAK FROM THE SOUTH

Plate 55

*November 27, 1838*

Roberts left Erment at 11 a.m. on November 26. He came in sight of Karnak two hours later, and landed near the great sanctuary after a few minutes. The next day he began to draw the ruins that had so impressed him a few weeks earlier. Although he was getting used to similar sights after having seen the Temple of Edfu, the Isle of Philae and the colossi of Rameses the Great at Abu Simbel, the ruins of ancient Thebes still filled him with awe. The impressions recorded in his journal on October 23 give an insight into his feelings, which were shared by all the intrepid travelers who sailed up the Nile to discover pharaonic Egypt in the 19th century. "Karnak is even more astonishing than Luxor. Its magnificence is unimaginable. Trying to describe rationally what I have seen would be ridiculous. The temple is so far removed from any previous experience of mine that I have nothing to compare it with. Like other Egyptian temples, at first sight it is actually a little disappointing, as the sanctuary stands in a huge plain which gives a misleading impression of its size; only as you draw closer to it are you astonished, indeed overcome by amazement. "You have to stand in their shadow, look up, and walk among these gigantic structures to understand; this frightens me, and my hand trembles at the thought that my drawings are unlikely to convey exactly what I mean. The columns are over 30 feet in circumference, so that a man looks like a pigmy beside them. The blocks that lie scattered all around are so huge that, even without considering how they were cut, it is impossible to imagine how they were brought here and put in their places."

# THE COLONNADE OF THE GREAT HYPOSTYLE ROOM IN THE TEMPLE OF KARNAK

Plate 56

*November 27, 1838*

*A*s already mentioned, Karnak and Luxor, with their famous temples, stand on the site of the ancient city of Thebes, several times the magnificent capital of the Egyptian empire and famous for its huge wealth. Homer described it in the ninth canto of the Iliad as the "city of a hundred gates" because of the countless caravans that arrived there every day, helping to increase the great economic and political power that came to dominate the area between the Sudan and the shores of the Mediterranean, Libya and Palestine. Founded as a modest fishing village in the Memphis period, Thebes grew enormously after the second unification of Upper and Lower Egypt; it reached the height of its glory between 1580 and 1085 BC. The great metropolis was dominated by the temple dedicated to the Theban Triad, which was extended and embellished by the pharaohs after each new victory against ever more distant enemies. Then, inexorably but unexpectedly, it fell into decline; the very geographical location that a thousand years earlier had led to its foundation and enhanced its power became the primary factor in its fall. Situated deep in the interior of the country, too far from the Mediterranean, which by then was becoming the center of the world, and from the Delta area, where the sovereigns of Rameses' dynasty had founded new military outposts against foreign invaders, Thebes rapidly lost its political and spiritual supremacy. Sais, Tanis and, finally, Bubastis, replaced Thebes as the imperial residence, beginning its decay. The Assyrian invasion, with the sack of Thebes by Assurbanipal in 672 BC, followed by the rule of the Ptolemies, finally condemned the city, so that by the time the Roman legions arrived, much of it had already fallen into ruin. During the Christian period many of the city's monuments were converted into churches and monasteries, while its works of art were scattered, or destroyed by those who viewed them as hideous symbols of paganism. Uaset (the Egyptian name of Thebes) was divided in half by a canal; the town of Luxor was founded to the south, while Karnak developed to the north. Despite the destruction and pillaging it has suffered, the Temple of Amun is still astonishing today for its extraordinary size, clearly depicted in the magnificent lithograph drawn by Roberts.

# THE NAVE OF THE GREAT HYPOSTYLE ROOM AT KARNAK

Plate 57

*November 28, 1838*

*T*his lithograph, like the previous one, shows a view of the hypostyle room in the Temple of Amun; this room, more than any other, left an indelible impression on Roberts's mind, and he drew it from various angles.

The great room, built by Seti I and Rameses II, can rightly be considered one of the wonders of the ancient world. In a total area of 6,000 square yards, 134 sandstone columns are aligned in 16 rows; the 12 that line the nave, shown in this lithograph, are over 80 feet tall, and are surmounted by capitals whose maximum circumference exceeds 50 feet. It is therefore not surprising that this room, the largest in the world to have a stone roof, was described by early archaeologists as a "forest of columns."

The considerable difference in height between the central columns and those in the aisles enabled numerous windows to be inserted between the architraves and the ceiling, thus ensuring that the room, enclosed by high walls on all sides, was adequately lit. One of these windows is clearly visible in the lithograph, at the top left. The slender obelisk of Thutmoses I, the only survivor of the four that the powerful pharaoh erected in the courtyard between the third and fourth pylons, can be seen in the background. Every surface is extensively decorated with bas-reliefs and inscriptions explaining the complex liturgical rites and the relationships between the sovereigns and the gods; sadly, the bright colors reproduced by Roberts have now faded in many places, or even disappeared.

Although Roberts usually portrayed his subjects faithfully, he made an exception in this lithograph. Probably fearing that he might embarrass some of the subscribers of the work, and even offend against the moral code of the period, he decided to censor the bas-reliefs portraying the immodest god Min, protector of fertility, who was represented by the ancient Egyptians as ithyphallic.

Thebes

Great Hall at Karnac Nov 29 1838.

David Roberts R.A. Louis Haghe Lith

143

# THE GREAT HYPOSTYLE ROOM AT KARNAK SEEN FROM THE EXTERIOR

Plate 58

*November 28, 1838*

*R*oberts spent four days at Karnak, working feverishly, as if obsessed by the idea that he would be unable to do justice to the magnificence of what was once the earthly dwelling of Amun, lord of the gods. He rose at dawn, and braving the heat and the tiresome bites of the ever-present mosquitos, continued drawing and taking measurements until twilight. Then he finally took a well-deserved rest, dining with two British travelers, Woolner Corry and William Hurnard, whom he had met earlier on his way to the Second Cataract. On the return journey the two had stopped at Karnak and, hearing that Roberts was there, decided to stay for a few days to visit ancient Thebes together with him. In his journal the Scotsman describes them as affable and good company.

The pair set off for Cairo on the evening of December 4. Corry's signature can still be seen carved in the stone of various Egyptian monuments, according to a deplorable custom that knows no limits of time or place. The lithograph shows another view of the hypostyle room, this time seen from the outside. Roberts's evident fondness for this room, which in our eyes may appear excessive, is justified by the fact that at the time, the remains of the sacred building appeared as a jumble of very badly damaged structures, partly buried in the sand, which were difficult to interpret as a whole.

Nearly all the pharaohs decided to extend the sanctuary, sometimes demolishing and re-using the previous constructions, with the result that the architecture of the building is highly complex, even after extensive restoration work, which began in the last century and has not yet been completed. The temple, which was called Ipet-isut, can be described as a theological treatise in stone, as it develops along two axes running from east to west and north to south, constituting mystical representations of sky and earth, divine power and royal power. It comprised four courtyards, ten pylons, a sacred lake and numerous associated buildings, including the Temple of Khonsu and a small sanctuary consecrated to Opet, the mother of Isis.

# VIEW OF THE RUINS OF KARNAK
## AT SUNRISE

Plate 59

*November 29, 1838*

*T*his large view of the Temple of Karnak, drawn at dawn on November 29, is one of the most successful in the entire collection both in its composition and in purely emotional terms; the ruins are bathed in the warm morning sunlight, while the group of local people portrayed in the foreground gives the scene a touch of romantic exoticism. In the background, from left to right, can be seen the first pylon of the huge religious complex, the column of Taharqa, the remains of the second pylon, the colonnade of the great hypostyle room, the obelisks

world. Begun under the sovereigns of the 12th dynasty, the huge building represents the result of over 16 centuries of work and extensions, which make it a kind of compendium of Egyptian art. As this was the largest center for the worship of Amun, it was very important for every sovereign to make improvements to it. Soon, because of the logic of its general proportions, extension required the erection of ever more colossal buildings; the result is this gigantic structure, full of repetitions and some degree of architectural

of Thutmoses I and Queen Hatshepsut, the banqueting hall of Thutmoses III and the portal of Nectanebo I. The view is expressly designed to highlight the immense size of the sanctuary which, with its area of 75 acres, is the largest column-supported temple in the

confusion, but undoubtedly unique. The Temple of Amun is the monument that, more than any other, represents the magnificence of the triumphal buildings erected by the pharaohs for religious reasons and to enhance their political prestige.

# THE GREAT COURTYARD OF KARNAK AND THE COLUMN OF TAHARQA

Plate 60

*November 29, 1838*

*T*he sacred complex of Karnak consists of three areas separated by enclosure walls made of air-dried bricks. In the main enclosure stand the great Temple of Amun and the smaller Temple of Khonsu, the moon god, who was considered the son of Amun and Mut in Thebes; on the left is the Sanctuary of Montu, the god of war, while on the opposite side, still largely unexplored, is the temple of the goddess Mut. Access to the Temple of Amun was originally obtained via two different routes, depending on whether visitors arrived from the Nile or overland. In both cases the entrance was announced by a row of tall pylons, each of which resembled two large trapezoidal towers framing a portal, probably inspired by military architecture. These characteristic structural elements are almost certainly the reason for the present name of Karnak, which in Arabic designates a fortified place. Worshippers arriving from the south walked down a long sphinx-lined avenue and entered through the south propylaea, which led to the courtyard enclosed between the third and fourth pylons, onto which the actual temple opened.

The main route, from the river, was perpendicular to the cella. After passing the first pylon, visitors entered the great courtyard, the largest in any of the Egyptian temples: built during the 22nd dynasty (945-745 BC), it is lined with 18 columns on the left and 9 on the right, all in the shape of closed scrolls. At the center of the huge area stands a column 70 feet tall, the only one surviving from a kiosk built by Ethiopian King Taharqa around 680 BC.

When Roberts explored the temple, the great courtyard was blocked by ruins, and only half of the huge column was above the surface, the rest being buried in the sand.

The courtyard leads to the great hypostyle room, which is followed, after the third and fourth pylons, by a room called the "small vestibule"; two more pylons precede the sacrarium, which is followed by the "banqueting hall."

149

# Transverse view of the great hypostyle room at Karnak

Plate 61

*November 29, 1838*

*This umpteenth view of the hypostyle room shows not only the gigantic proportions of the columns by comparison with the Lilliputian figures that appear at the foot of one of them, but also the badly damaged condition of the building. Roberts also emphasized the extraordinary complexity of the bright, polychrome decorations of the temple. During the thousand-year history of the sanctuary, whole generations of sovereigns left their mark by covering every available surface with hieroglyphics and figures. These bas-reliefs not only illustrate the religious beliefs of the ancient Egyptians in great detail, but also contain a wealth of invaluable references to historical events in the country. The information provided by the Temple of Karnak has enabled the exact chronology of the events that took place during the New Kingdom to be reconstructed, and a complete list of the successive sovereigns who built the sanctuary to be drawn up. None of them spared any expense: an inscription recalls that Queen Hatshepsut lavished on the temple "as many bushels of gold as sacks of corn." During the 19th dynasty (1335–1205 BC) over 80,000 men worked at the temple, including manual workers, peasants, slaves, watchmen and priests. In order to understand the enthusiasm for construction work of these followers of Amun, it should be remembered that the worship of the lord of the gods had*

*received its official consecration at Karnak, supported by a magnificent liturgy far removed from the simple, spontaneous faith of the people.*
*Around 2000 BC Amun was beginning to be considered the supreme being by all those who recognized the authority of the pharaoh, often associated with the image of the god.*

*The development of the sanctuary into the greatest religious center in Egypt, which involved countless renovations, completely changed the original appearance of the sacred complex, although it still retained the basic characteristics of the Egyptian temple, considered the "palace" of the god on earth.*

151

# THE RUINS OF THE TEMPLE OF MEDAMOUT NEAR KARNAK

Plate 62

*November 30, 1838*

The inclusion of this lithograph in our book presented a real puzzle, because Roberts never made any explicit mention of the Temple of Medamout during either the outward or the return journey. However, on the basis of some practical considerations, it is reasonable to assume that the artist visited the site on November 30. His journal shows that during the previous three days he was engaged in drawing the Temple of Karnak, of which he notes that he made seven drawings, probably the same ones that appear in the previous pages (including the frontispiece of this chapter, portaying the great portal erected by Ptolemy III). On Saturday, December 1, he wrote that he had "started and finished at Luxor," and on Sunday, in observance of Biblical precepts, he did no work, but merely visited Medinet Abu. From that time until his departure for Dendera on the evening of the 6th he stayed on the left bank of the Nile where the funeral temples, the Colossi of Memnon and the Valley of the Kings are situated. That only leaves November 30, about which he vaguely wrote that he had drawn some sketches and made two studies in oils. The Temple of Medamout is situated just under four miles north of Karnak, on the same bank; at the time the area was not encumbered by modern buildings, and the ruins must have been easily visible, representing a great attraction for the untiring Roberts. We therefore hope that we are not mistaken in our supposition, but if we are, we trust that readers will excuse our long digression.

The remains of the Temple of Montu, still visible today at Medamout, date back to the Ptolemaic and Roman age, although the origins of the sanctuary are far more remote. In ancient Madu (the original name of the place) the worship of the war god began during the Old Kingdom, when the first temple was founded. This temple was later extended by Sesostris III and, when the importance of the war god increased, by the sovereigns of the New Kingdom. During the three centuries of Ptolemaic rule in Egypt, a large number of existing sanctuaries were restored and new ones consecrated to the ancient lords of the Egyptian pantheon, and it was in this context that the temple was renovated.

All that now remains of the building are the five columns drawn by Roberts; the two flanking the great portal are surmounted by richly decorated capitals with floral motifs, while the others are the fascicular papyrus type with closed capitals.

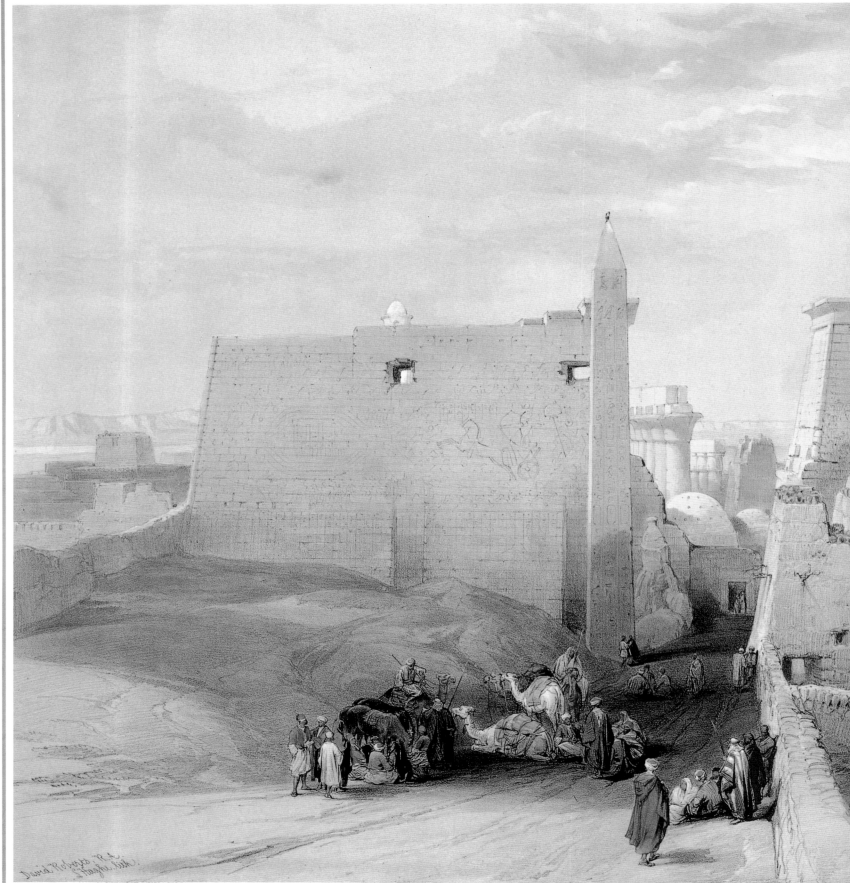

# THE FAÇADE OF THE GREAT TEMPLE OF AMUN AT LUXOR

Plate 63

*December 1, 1838*

*Grand Entrance to the Temple of Luxor*

Roberts stayed only one day, December 1, at Luxor; this suggests that he had already made various sketches during the outward journey, which he then completed on the basis of new observations. While he was working on the preparatory drawing for this lithograph, a falcon perched on the top of the obelisk facing the great pylon of the temple. Every so often the bird took off and swooped on the intrusive pigeons surrounding the artist, who scattered in terror. As if to express his thanks, Roberts included the bird in his view. The great sanctuary, half buried by debris, was suffocated by a myriad of shacks, with hundreds of earthenware pots used as dovecotes on their roofs. A building surmounted by a dome can be seen in the first courtyard, while the summit of the minaret of the Mosque of Abu el-Haggag, which still stands inside the archaeological site, appears behind the left-hand tower. The temple was only dug out in 1885 by French archaeologist Gaston Maspéro, who began the large-scale excavations that are still continuing.

# The Obelisk of Rameses II at Luxor

Plate 64

*December 1, 1838*

The temple of Luxor was the main satellite of the huge sacred complex of Karnak, to which it was connected under Nectanebo I by a majestic avenue of human-headed sphinxes almost two miles long. A monumental site already existed in this part of Thebes in the Middle Kingdom, as confirmed by the reuse of older materials; however, the architectural history of the Luxor sanctuary is far more unified than that of Karnak. The present building was erected under only three pharaohs: Amenhotep III, Tutankhamen and Rameses II. The first, in the 14th century BC, commissioned the design from Amenhotep son of Hapu, famous for his wisdom and worshipped as a god after his death, who unusually oriented the temple from north to south so as to connect it directly with Amun's dwelling at Karnak. As was the usual practice, his two successors extended the temple and repeated the same structural elements. The original layout included the naos preceded by the hypostyle room, while the courtyard surrounded by porticoes and the great colonnade were added later by the Amenhotep III. On his death, his son Akhenaton the Heretic (Amenhotep IV) abandoned the project and left the capital to found a new cult of Aton and a new imperial city, the present Tell el-Amarna; the monument was later completed by his son-in-law Tutankhamen who, after returning to Thebes and the religion of his ancestors, wished to prove his faith by making numerous embellishments. During the 19th dynasty Rameses II completed the temple by adding the great colonnaded courtyard with the axis towards the east, preceded by the huge front pylon decorated with reliefs portraying his victory against the Hittites at the battle of Kadesh. In front of it he erected two obelisks, covered with propitiatory inscriptions and scenes of offerings to Amun, which were donated to France by the Pasha of Egypt Mohammed Ali. The western obelisk, standing over 70 feet tall and weighing 240 tons, was taken to Paris and erected by engineer Jean Baptiste Lebas in the middle of Place de la Concorde on October 25, 1836. Roberts, who strongly disapproved of this pillage, would probably have been pleased to hear that the French government officially renounced its right to ownership of the second obelisk in 1980.

# ONE OF THE COLOSSI OF RAMESES II IN FRONT OF THE TEMPLE OF LUXOR

*December 1, 1838*

Plate 65

*I*n addition to the two obelisks, six huge statues, half of which have been lost, originally faced the pylon of the temple. Roberts was only able to see the busts of the two dark granite colossi guarding the entrance, which emerged from the debris. The 50-foot-tall colossi both portrayed Rameses II seated on the throne, but the faces were already disfigured. The third huge statue, which can now be seen in front of the right-hand tower, was at that time buried under the sand; carved in red granite, it also portrays the pharaoh, but in a standing position. A cartouche containing some hieroglyphics can be seen on the right shoulder of the colossus. It is interesting in this respect to see that on a number of occasions Roberts expressed some doubt in his journal as to whether the ancient Egyptian language could really be deciphered. For example, on October 22, during his first visit to the Valley of the Kings, he wrote, "If it is true that hieroglyphics can be read, in this tomb it will certainly be possible to discover the entire pantheon of Egyptian mythology." Yet Jean François Champollion had published his Précis du système hiéroglyphique *in 1822, and by 1838 his method was universally recognized despite harsh criticism from English scientist Thomas Young, who also tried to solve the enigma but with no valid result.*

One of Two Colossal Statues of Ramases II. Entrance to the Temple of Luxor.

at Luxor, Thebes, Upper Egypt.

# THE COLONNADE OF THE COURTYARD OF AMENHOTEP III AT LUXOR

Plate 66

*December 1, 1838*

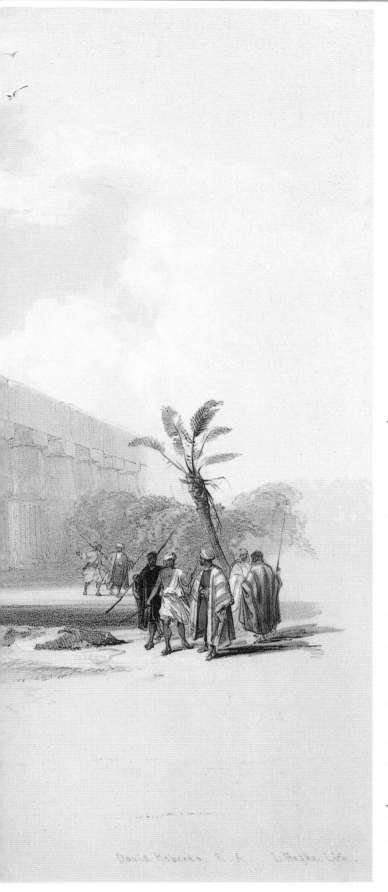

This lithograph shows a view of the colonnaded courtyard of Amenhotep III, a huge open space measuring 168 feet wide by 149 feet long, surrounded on three sides by two rows of closed-capital fascicular columns. At the time when Roberts made the drawing, this part of the temple was also half-buried, and many of the columns had fallen to the ground and were totally covered with sand. The temple of Luxor, which was called Ipet-resit (southern harem of Amun) had a very complex function. Every year during the Lovely Festival of Opet, celebrated in the second or third month of the flood season, the effigy of Amun was removed from the great temple of Karnak and placed on the sacred boat in a magnificent ceremony. Following a rigid hierarchy, the craft was followed by three other sacred boats; the first carried the statue of Mut, wife of Amun, the second the statue of their son Khonsu, and the third the pharaoh in person. The procession sailed slowly up the Nile as far as the temple of Luxor, which was situated on such high ground that it was never underwater even during the greatest floods. The statues were taken from the vessels and placed on symbolic boats shouldered by the priests; they passed the entrance pylon, advanced between the columns of the sanctuary, and were finally placed in the naos. The ritual boats, each placed in a different cella, were only removed ten days later; in the meantime Amun, by consecrating his mystic and carnal union with Mut, once again fertilized the world. At the same time, in the twilight of the most secret chambers of the temple, the pharaoh met the queen. During the festival the people, invited to manifest their joy, flocked from all over the region, while votive offerings poured incessantly into the temple, and were all the more plentiful if the harvest had been good. Women desiring children made pilgrimages to the sanctuary to invoke the aid and protection of Amun, honored in the guise of Min, whose erect phallus promised fertility. On the tenth day the statues were again placed in the boats, and the procession returned to Karnak. The pharaoh, regenerated and confirmed in his royal role, could then guarantee the prosperity of his people for another year, certain that the next harvest would be plentiful thanks to the benevolent influence of Amun.

# THE WEST BANK OF THE NILE SEEN FROM LUXOR

<u>Plate 67</u>

*December 1, 1838*

In order to make this drawing, Roberts had to scale one of the architraves of the colonnade surrounding the courtyard of Rameses II in the Temple of Luxor. From that privileged position the eye could range freely over the verdant plain that occupies the west bank of the Nile, where the pharaohs of the New Kingdom built their funeral temples. From left to right can be seen the temple of Rameses III at Medinet Habu, the solitary figures of the colossi of Memnon, the Ramesseum and the temple of Sethi I, near which stood the village of Goorna, now known as Qurnah. Behind the village lies the Valley of the Kings, where 62 royal tombs have so far been rescued from centuries of oblivion.

The powerful sovereigns of the Memphis period revolutionized Egyptian architecture by building pyramids to house their eternal dwelling-places, while Theban Pharaoh Thutmoses I (who reigned from 1525 to 1512 BC, at the beginning of the 18th dynasty) made the equally innovative decision to separate the mortuary temple from the actual sepulchre. This design greatly interested his successors, who trusted in the inviolability of their tombs to ensure that their journey to the afterlife would not be disturbed by grave robbers. Aligned along the Nile, not far from the entrance to the valley, stood the temples in honor of Amenhotep I, II and III, Merneptah and Merneptah-Sipta, Rameses I, II, III and IV, Sethi I and Thutmoses II, III and IV. The only survivors of these splendid buildings, which the pharaohs of three dynasties consecrated to the Theban Triad and their own worship, are those made of stone, while all the others, made of air-dried brick, have practically disappeared. Roberts did not include the temple of Queen Hatshepsut in the valley of Deir el-Bahari in the view; in fact, reconstruction work on the magnificent terraced complex, which can now easily be seen even from Luxor, was only commenced in 1967.

Entrance of the Temple of Amun of Luxor

# A GROUP OF EGYPTIANS IN THE TEMPLE OF SETI I AT THEBES

Plate 68

*December 3, 1838*

*R*oberts spent the first Sunday in December visiting the neighborhood of the village of Qurnah, probably with Hurnard and Corry, abstaining from work on the Sabbath. The next day he started work again with a will, and was already on his way to the Valley of the Kings in the early hours of the morning. During the journey he stopped briefly at the ruins of the mortuary temple of Seti I, which stands in the plain of Thebes on the edge of the fertile area. Built on the foundations of a previous building, the impressive structure was dedicated by the pharaoh to the god Amun with the intention of perpetuating his own memory and honoring that of his father, Rameses I. The sovereign, who reigned from 1306 to 1290 BC, did not live to see the temple completed; it was finished by his successor Rameses II.

The great complex is now badly damaged; little remains of the first and second pylons, or of the two huge courtyards. All that remains of the long processional avenue that led to the temple are two sphinxes, while the portico that closed the second courtyard to the east, behind the smaller pylon, still has nine of the ten original fascicular columns. Three portals connect the portico to the corresponding sectors of the temple dedicated to the three sovereigns, in accordance with a very unusual layout. The central hypostyle room, surrounded by numerous secondary rooms used as stores for boats and sacred articles, leads to the actual naos, the ceiling of which rested on four pillars. The chapels of Rameses I and Rameses II and their ancillary rooms have unfortunately been badly damaged.

The background to the scene portrayed by Roberts in this lithograph is a section of the portico, which provided refreshing shade for some very picturesque characters. In front of the water pipe in the center sits one of the pasha's officials, who had come to Qurnah to collect taxes and adjudicate on any disputes relating to the actions of local administrators; on his right is the village sheik, accompanied by an attendant. Some local dignitaries are waiting their turn, probably to buy the official's favors with gifts and offerings, as corruption was rife at this period. Fascinated by exotic scenes as always, Roberts also included the figure of a veiled woman and two children, whose clothes indicated that they belonged to different classes.

# The Valley of the Kings

Plate 69

*December 3, 1838*

*After leaving the Temple of Seti I, Roberts went on to the Valley of the Kings. When the artist paid his first visit to the valley on October 22, he made no drawings but merely took notes on the most interesting tombs, especially that of Seti I, discovered by Belzoni 21 years earlier. The undulating Valley of the Kings, surrounded by overhanging rocks, stretches sinuously along the foot of Mount el-Qurn, also known as the Theban Heights, whose triangular shape is reminiscent of a pyramid. Here lie the tombs of the pharaohs of the 18th, 19th and 20th dynasties. The Arabic name of the place, Biban el-Moluk (The Kings' Doors) alludes to the entrances of these sepulchres, which were excavated in the calcareous rock. As already mentioned, the Valley of the Kings was destined to become one of the most famous archaeological sites in the world as a result of an original decision by Thutmoses I who, breaking with a tradition 17 centuries old, decided to separate his eternal resting place from the funeral temple and conceal it in a well-protected place.*

*The pharaoh's architect Ineni excavated a well-type tomb in the inaccessible rock wall of the valley, and placed a burial chamber at the end of it to receive the sarcophagus of the deceased and his burial objects. This inaugurated the typical design of the royal tomb, which was gradually developed by his successors with the addition of corridors, hypostyle rooms and secondary rooms. After the mortal remains of the pharaoh had been buried, the tomb was never visited again, as the royal cult continued in the funeral temples situated in the plain on the edge of the cultivated areas. Contrary to common belief, the accesses to the tombs were not secret; in fact, the guardians of the valley periodically checked the seals affixed at the time of burial. Sadly, this precaution was insufficient to protect the luxurious burial objects from tomb robbers, who often acted in partnership with the guards. Two papyrus scrolls and other written documents record violations of the tombs as early as the 20th dynasty; later, nearly all the tombs were pillaged, and the Theban priests had to conceal the mummies of many pharaohs in a secret hiding place, which was not discovered until 1881.*

*The only tomb that was not violated was that of Tutankhamen with its fabulous treasure, discovered by Howard Carter and Lord Carnarvon in 1922. Oddly, Roberts only drew a panoramic view of the valley, with the entrances to the tombs that could then be seen, neglecting the spectacular interior decorations he had been so excited about. However, the lithograph is of some interest because it shows the artist himself together with Hurnard, Corry, Ismail and Hassan Amoris.*

Deir el Medineh Thebes

# THE TEMPLE OF PTOLEMY IV AT DEIR EL-MEDINA

Plate 70

*December 3, 1838*

he road that now winds through the Valley of the Kings follows the route used in ancient times to take the royal sarcophagi from Thebes to their last abode. The men who worked on the construction of the tombs and lived in the village of Deir el-Medina went to work by a much shorter route, still easily followed, which crosses the ridge between the two parallel valleys. After exploring the tombs Roberts preferred to take this shorter footpath back to Qurnah, and it soon led him to the place where the builders of the royal necropolis had lived. Nearby stood a very well preserved small temple, built by Ptolemy IV Philopator in honor of Hathor and Maat, the patron deities of Theban sepulchres; the small sanctuary was also consecrated to architects Imhotep and Amenhotep. The former had designed the first pyramid in Egypt, at Djoser, while the latter built the temple of Luxor under Amenhotep III; in accordance with the complicated syncretism of the Egyptian religion, both of these historical figures were later deified, thus entering the huge pantheon presided over by Amun-Ra. The building, completed by Ptolemy VII Evergete II, has a regular plan; the hypostyle atrium, whose ceiling is now missing, is followed by a small vestibule onto which the doors of three adjacent chapels open.

The architrave of the vestibule is supported by two columns with magnificent floral patterns and two attractive Hathor pillars; the window seen in the lithograph shed light on a staircase leading to the terraced roof. The building is very small: less than 30 feet wide by 45 feet long.

The very well balanced proportions of the whole and the exquisite workmanship of the decorations justify the attention devoted to it by Roberts, who in this illustration portrayed himself at work, exotically dressed in the Turkish style, as was then customary in Egypt.

Statues of Memnon. Thebes. Decr 4th 1838

David Roberts, R.A. L. Haghe

# The Colossi of Memnon in the plain of Thebes

Plate 71

*December 4, 1838*

Roberts spent the whole of December 4, drawing the Colossi of Memnon from three different angles. These huge twin statues, already famous in ancient times, are all that remains of the funeral temple of Amenhotep III, the largest in western Thebes, designed by the architect Amenhotep. The building, situated in the easternmost part of the alluvial plain of the Nile, was largely made of air-dried bricks and almost certainly undermined by the annual floods of the river. It was eventually reduced to a heap of rubble, and used by the pharaoh's successors as a source of building material. A similar fate was suffered by the pharaoh's magnificent palace at Malqatta, a few miles northeast of the temple.

The great palace, protected by a massive enclosure wall inside of which there were also numerous food stores, stood opposite the huge reservoir of Birket Abu, connected to the Nile by a navigable canal. The only remaining signs of its bygone glory are the two statues portraying the deified Amenhotep III, which originally stood on either side of the entrance portal of the temple. Carved in the very hard siliceous sandstone from the Edfu quarries, they have withstood continual erosion and still survive today. The outline of the funeral temple of Rameses III at Medinet Habu can be seen in the background of the lithograph.

# THE COLOSSI OF MEMNON
## SEEN FROM THE SOUTHWEST

Plate 72

*December 4, 1838*

*B*oth of the huge statues of Amenhotep III, called the Colossi of Memnon by Greek travelers because of a mistaken interpretation of the Egyptian name, were damaged by an earthquake in 27 BC that also probably inflicted the finishing blow on the temple behind them. After the earthquake, the northern statue began to emit a characteristic wailing sound when it was heated by the rays of the rising sun. This increased the popularity of the colossi and strengthened the legend, dating from the Ptolemaic period, that identified them with Homer's hero Memnon, slain by Achilles beneath the walls of Troy, whose effigy received the beneficial caresses of his mother Aurora every morning with a gentle moan. The Colossi of Memnon became the most popular monuments in Egypt, and in Roman times attracted hordes of travelers, who also admired their huge size. Including the bases, the two statues are just under 65 feet tall. The bas-reliefs that can still be seen on the sides of the thrones depict the two Nile divinities entwining a lotus and a papyrus, the heraldic plants of Upper and Lower Egypt, symbolizing the union of the two kingdoms. Statues of Amenhotep's mother, Mutemuia, stand on the left-hand side of the legs of each colossus, and those of his wife, Teie, on the right. In the scene portrayed by Roberts, Hurnard, Corry and Hassan Amoris, who accompanied him on his excursion, are scaling the "wailing" colossus with the aid of a rope.

# The Colossi of Memnon at Sunrise

Plate 73

*December 4, 1838*

*D*uring the first two centuries AD, visiting the Colossi of Memnon at Thebes became fashionable among Greek and Roman travelers. Already mentioned by Strabo, the phenomenon of the wailing statue was confirmed by Pausania and Juvenal in the 2nd century AD. Numerous Greek and Latin inscriptions can still be read on the lower part of the northern statue, demonstrating that it was only this one that produced the strange lament; they include inscriptions by poet Julia Balbilla, who accompanied the Emperor Hadrian and his wife, Sabina, on their trip to Egypt, and by the Greek poet Asklepiodotos. Unfortunately, the sound entirely ceased when Septimius Severus, perhaps to alleviate the anguish of Memnon, restored the colossus and rebuilt the upper part. This lithograph, in which the colossi are bathed in the light of the rising sun reflected on the flooded plain, represents a good example of the virtuoso technique and romantic spirit of the artist, who reached heights of true lyricism, although the scene was artificially constructed. In fact, the floods of the Nile began between May and June and increased until early October, after which they decreased rapidly; Roberts could not, therefore, have witnessed this event.

**From David Roberts's journal:**

*December 5 - Today I was particularly busy, mainly because of a furious storm, a very rare event in these parts. I made two large drawings of the Memnonium and two of the Temple of Medinet Abou.*

# THE RAMESSEUM AT THEBES
## DURING A STORM

Plate 74

*December 5, 1838*

On December 5, a violent thunderstorm broke unexpectedly. The ancient ruins stood out clearly against the Theban plain like apparitions, illuminated by spectral flashes of lightning as the sky grew darker and darker. Fascinated by this scene of wild beauty, Roberts decided to take advantage of the rare opportunity of drawing the funeral temple of Rameses II in the storm. Although it has suffered ill treatment at the hands of man and the elements, the great building, which Champollion baptized the Ramesseum, is one of the most perfect and elegant examples of this architectural style. The temple was already famous in classical antiquity; historian Diodorus Siculus wrote a marvelling description of it, and it was also mentioned by Greek geographer Strabo, although he called it the Memnonium because Rameses was incorrectly identified with the legendary Ethiopian King Memnon, son of Eos (Aurora) and Tithonos, slain during the Trojan War. The Ramesseum originally consisted of a number of buildings surrounded by an outer wall of sun-dried bricks, namely the temple for royal worship where the glories of the pharaoh were celebrated with great pomp, a minor sanctuary dedicated to his mother and wife, the great stores containing the provisions required for the liturgy and the sustenance of the priests, and the royal palace where Rameses himself resided during the ceremonies.

Although the term "funeral temple" is now in common use, this variety of functions suggests that it is incorrect; in fact, these magnificent buildings were used by the pharaohs while they were still alive. Associated with the worship of the deified sovereign and with the god Amun, the chief Theban deity, they were called Million-Year Castles by the ancient Egyptians. The pharaohs celebrated there a festival of very ancient origin that, formally, was held during the thirtieth year of their reign in order to regenerate their strength and that of the whole country. The elaborate purification rites and offerings needed to aid the reunion of the deceased with the supreme deity only began on the death of the sovereign, in the silence of these temples.

# THE COLOSSUS OF RAMESES II IN THE RAMESSEUM

Plate 75

*December 5, 1838*

*L*ike all travelers who visited the ruins of the Ramesseum, Roberts was astonished by the fragments of the colossus of Rameses the Great. The huge statue, made by order of the pharaoh in his own likeness and placed in front of the second pylon of the temple, was originally just under 60 feet tall. Made of a single block of red Aswan granite weighing over 1100 tons, it portrayed the sovereign seated on his throne, with the double crown of Upper and Lower Egypt on his head. The pharaoh's name is still easily visible on the cartouches carved on the forearms and seat. The colossus inspired Shelley's famous sonnet Ozymandias; this name derives from the Greek translation of Rameses II's forename, Usermaatra (Powerful is the Truth of Ra). Many theories have been postulated to explain the destruction of this wonder of the ancient world, including the earthquake that devastated the region in 27 BC, but the responsibility for the damage probably lies with the Coptic Christians, who considered any image associated with the ancient Egyptian religion to be blasphemous. On the left of the huge fragmentary bust stand four Osiris pillars surviving from the portico that ran around the second courtyard of the temple; behind them can be seen the few remains of the second pylon. The ruins of the first pylon, decorated on the right-hand side with a bas-relief depicting Rameses II on his battle chariot as he stops the advance of the Hittites, can be seen in the background. In the left foreground lie fragments of the two impressive statues of the pharaoh that stood guard over the large hypostyle room; the splendid head of one of them, called the Young Memnon, was recovered by Giovanni Battista Belzoni in 1816 and conveyed to the British Museum. The Ramesseum was one of the most monumental works ordered by Rameses the Great, an enterprising, determined sovereign sometimes identified with the pharaoh of the Exodus, who left signs of frenetic construction work all over Egypt and Nubia. Abandoned at the end of the 20th dynasty, the temple was later used as a burial place for Theban priests, then as a source of building materials, and finally as a Coptic church; it has undergone extensive restoration work in recent years.

Fragment of the Great Colossus, at the Memnonium, Thebes

# THE TEMPLE OF MEDINET HABU AT THEBES

Plate 76

*December 5, 1838*

Not far from the Ramesseum, at Medinet Habu, stand the spectacular ruins of the mortuary temple built by Rameses III in an area occupied by some older sacred buildings. Roberts had already admired the great complex during his previous visit on October 21. "We then visited the temple of Medinet Habu, which of all those standing on the west bank of Thebes is the most extraordinary, beyond description."

The sanctuary area is bounded by a mighty enclosure wall of sun-dried bricks, in the south side of which opens the lovely South Gate, set between two tall towers, which the archaeologists in Napoleon's entourage renamed The Pavilion. This unusual structure (the tallest part of the building visible in the lithograph) is entirely covered with bas-reliefs, mainly of a military nature, glorifying the figure of the pharaoh.

On the right-hand side of the pavilion stands the temple of Thutmoses II: two slender columns surmounted by capitals in the shape of open scrolls precede an elegant portal dominated by a winged solar disk. The mortuary temple of Rameses III, which stood inside a second enclosure wall that has now practically disappeared, is one of the most stylistically perfect surviving specimens of Egyptian architecture.

Two courtyards, each preceded by a tall pylon, follow one after another along the southwest northeast axis; these are followed, again in a straight line, by a roofed part constituted by three hypostyle rooms, and finally the naos. The ruins of the royal palace, consisting of a hypostyle audience chamber, the throne room and numerous service rooms, can still be seen on the left-hand side of the temple.

Archaeological excavations have also uncovered traces of a town built around the palace, but only the home of an inspector of the Theban necropolises has remained sufficiently intact to be recognizable. The openings of what are known as the Tombs of the Nobility, excavated in spurs of rock bounding the Theban plain, are recognizable on the right side of the lithograph. Here, as in two other similar necropolises, court dignitaries, priests and high-ranking soldiers were buried during the Middle Kingdom.

# Ruins of a Coptic church in the Temple of Medinet Habu

Plate 77

*December 5, 1838*

Following the edict issued in 383 AD by the Emperor Theodosius which proclaimed Christianity to be the sole religion allowed in the Roman Empire, many Egyptian temples were converted into churches. At Medinet Habu, the sanctuary of Rameses III actually became the center of a large Coptic village that prospered until the Arab conquest of Egypt in the 7th century. The remains of this village, demolished from 1858 onwards during excavations begun by Auguste

supported by porphyry columns surmounted by Corinthian capitals, which Roberts saw still standing and portrayed in his view. As these remains were removed during the excavation and restoration of the mortuary temple, the lithograph is now of great historical value.
The second courtyard has been restored to its original appearance, and is now surrounded by porticoes on all sides; to the north and south are the traditional Osiris pillars, badly damaged by the Christian monks, and to the east and west

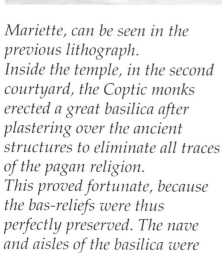

Mariette, can be seen in the previous lithograph.
Inside the temple, in the second courtyard, the Coptic monks erected a great basilica after plastering over the ancient structures to eliminate all traces of the pagan religion.
This proved fortunate, because the bas-reliefs were thus perfectly preserved. The nave and aisles of the basilica were

ten columns in the shape of closed scrolls. The reliefs decorating the end walls show battle scenes, clearly for propaganda purposes, or scenes of ostentatious religious devotion depicting the procession following the sacred boat, the apparition of the god Min, the exit of the pharaoh from the palace and his entry into the temple.

# THE INTERIOR OF THE TEMPLE OF DENDERA

Plate 78

*December 6, 1838*

Roberts took his leave of ancient Thebes on the afternoon of December 5, and thanks to the favorable wind that enabled the crew to unfurl the sails for the first time since Abu Simbel, was in Dendera by 11 o'clock the next morning. He set to work enthusiastically, enraptured by the majesty of the Temple of Hathor. The great sanctuary exercised an indelible fascination on his mind, almost amounting to a spell, as demonstrated by the huge canvas now in the Bristol City Art Gallery, painted in oils in 1841 from sketches made locally. Dendera, originally called Tentyris, was one of the most important religious centers in ancient Egypt. The city was rendered sacred by three sanctuaries: the Sanctuary of Horus, god of the sky and protector of the pharaohs, the Sanctuary of Ihy, the young sistrum-playing son of Horus, and the Sanctuary of Hathor. Only the latter has survived practically intact, while no more than a few traces remain of the other two. Like Roberts, all the European travelers and archaeologists who made their way to the heart of Upper Egypt in the last century were deeply enchanted by the temple consecrated to the goddess of love and pleasure; at the time of Roberts's visit the building was half-buried in the sand, but it already emanated the charm that is now manifested in all its splendor as a result of extensive excavation and restoration work. When researchers and draftsmen began systematic exploration of the ruins, it soon became clear that the southern orientation of the temple and the great mask of Hathor on the south wall had a precise meaning; several miles lower down on the same bank of the Nile stands the temple of Edfu, dedicated to Horus, husband of the gentle goddess worshipped at Dendera. The two sites were the major centers of worship of these deities, and were linked by a mystic twinship that culminated every May in a great festival during which the effigies of Horus and Hathor were taken in procession along the Nile in sacred boats to recall their divine union. Since the most ancient times Dendera must have had a sanctuary, that was destroyed and rebuilt several times; however, the present complex dates from the late Ptolemaic and Roman period. This explains the prevalence of a magnificently scenic style, less severe than that of the oldest Egyptian temples, clearly evident in this lithograph, which shows the interior of the first hypostyle room, a magnificent chamber over 80 feet deep, featuring 18 huge columns covered with bas-reliefs.

**From David Roberts's journal:**

*December 6 - Today I drew the interior of the temple, the best preserved in all Egypt, which far surpasses all the others in the variety and quality of its reliefs. Although they are rather late, to my eyes they have all the majestic grandeur and effective simplicity of the older ones.*

View from under the Portico
of the Temple of Dendera.

David Roberts R.A.

# THE FAÇADE OF THE TEMPLE OF HATHOR AT DENDERA

Plate 79

*December 7, 1838*

*T*he temple of Dendera does not feature the pylon usually present in sacred Egyptian architecture; the front of the building is formed by a massive structure measuring 139 feet wide by 60 feet high, with six columns on the façade on which an impressive cornice rests. The intercolumniations are occupied as far as halfway up by panels covered with hieroglyphic texts and bas-reliefs, while the entrance opens in the center, forming a high, empty space wider than the adjacent ones. Inside, 18 more columns stand in three rows; all the capitals reproduced the features of the patron goddess of the place. As it is higher than the rest of the temple, this hypostyle room, added under Tiberius, to some extent acts as the missing pylon. The whole building, with its markedly trapezoidal shape and massive columns, might appear graceless and even unharmonious, but the perfect balance between solid and hollow effects and the minute details of the rich ornamentation are some of the features that make it an architectural miracle. Roberts was evidently somewhat awestruck by this miracle, as by his own admission he spent much of December 7, looking for the right angle from which to make his drawing.

Despite the hesitation he expressed about the success of his work, the drawing is very high quality, and gives very good insight into Roberts's outstanding technique, here splendidly enhanced by the craftsmanship of Louis Haghe. The descriptive detail of one is emphasized by the meticulous sensitivity of the other in a symbiosis rarely equaled for evocative power and the success of the aesthetic result.

As in the previous lithograph, the almost obsessive attention to reproducing even the smallest details is quite incredible. It is therefore a real tragedy that the fury of the Coptic monks, who had converted the temple into a church, was mainly unleashed against the images of Hathor, a young woman with an enigmatic smile; Roberts regretted that he could not draw the huge capitals as they once were, decorated with the lovely face of the goddess, now pathetically disfigured. Fortunately, the colors were still vivid, especially on the ceiling of the hypostyle room and the column drums.

# THE KIOSK OF ISIS ON THE ROOF OF THE TEMPLE OF DENDERA

Plate 80

*December 8, 1838*

As they were associated by the worship of Hathor and Horus and built at almost the same time, the temples of Edfu and Dendera present some very similar architectural features. Although they are both very well preserved, only the one consecrated to the goddess has the "irradiation chapel" still intact, at the southwest corner of the terraced roof. Once a year the sacred image, usually kept in the naos, was brought here and exposed to the sunlight to be regenerated. The procession of priests followed a long staircase cut in the left-hand embankment, the walls of which are decorated with figures going up one way and down the other, showing how the ceremony was performed. The kiosk where the rite of presentation to the sun god Ra was performed is an elegant peripteral building with 12 Hathor columns, connected halfway up by the usual curtain walls. In the northern part of the terrace stands a small chapel dedicated to Osiris, which was probably choked with sand and debris when Roberts saw it.

After Abydos, Dendera was the most important of the sanctuaries containing the 14 parts of the body of the god, cut to pieces by the cruel Seth. This importance was due to Hathor's associations with Osiris and Horus. In Egyptian cosmogony the goddess Hathor (whose name literally means "house of the god Horus"), daughter of Isis, at some point began to be identified with her mother, who had generated Horus by coupling with part of her husband's corpse after regenerating the phallus with her magic arts. Thus the two eventually came to be considered one and the same. Isis, daughter of Ra and mother of Horus and Ihy, goddess of nature and magic, was the wife of Osiris, the god of death and resurrection; she searched for the parts of his body scattered by Seth along the Nile Valley, and buried them in various sacred places. This explains the complex relationship and the reasons for what might be called the cross-worship between Dendera and Edfu.

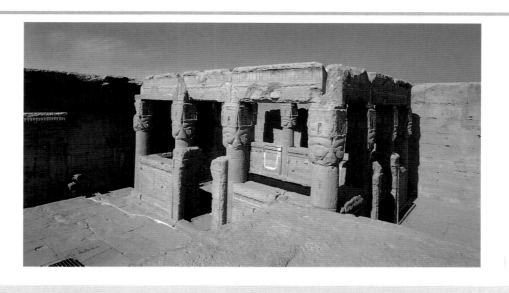

Dendera — Dec.ʳ 1838

# THE GREAT ENTRANCE PORTAL TO THE SACRED ENCLOSURE OF DENDERA

Plate 81

*December 8, 1838*

The Temple of Dendera, built by Ptolemy IX Soter II, stands in the middle of a huge area bounded by a wall of air-dried bricks, almost entirely ruined, whose sides are between 925 and 990 feet long; on the north and east sides are two magnificent portals built during the period of Roman rule. Roberts drew the one facing east, the best preserved; as is clear from the lithograph, much of the structure was buried at the time, as were the Temple of Hathor and the other buildings surrounding it.

Apart from the great sanctuary, some outstanding monuments stand in the sacred enclosure. Not far from the rear façade of the great temple are the badly damaged remains of a small sanctuary dedicated to the birth of Isis; the surviving reliefs portray Nut, goddess of the sky, giving birth while sitting on a stool in accordance with the ancient local custom. Nearby, to the west, is a deep rectangular hollow enclosed by a boundary wall; this is all that remains of the sacred lake typical of all Egyptian sanctuaries, where the priests had to perform their ritual ablutions several times a day. The most interesting remains, including a well, a sanatorium dating from the Roman period, a Coptic church and two mammisi, one Ptolemaic and the other Roman, are scattered along the western wall and in the northwest corner of the Temple of Hathor. The Roman mammisi, incorrectly called the Typhonium, appears in the lithograph shown in Plate 9 of this volume, which was probably drawn, or at least sketched, on October 20, as Roberts made no reference to it during his second visit. Mammisi, whose name literally means birth chapel, are small temples typical of the Early Period in which the pharaohs' children were honored on the pretext of worshipping the birth of the gods. Their children, considered to be on a par with living deities, could only be born within the sacred precincts of the temple. The first building of this kind was erected at Dendera by Nectanebo I between 378 and 360 BC, while the adjacent one was built by order of Augustus.

After taking leave of Henry Tattam, one of the most famous Egyptologists of the day, whom he had met on his arrival at Dendera, Roberts decided that he was satisfied with the work he had done, and recommenced his journey on the evening of December 8.

# THE NILE NEAR THE PYRAMIDS OF DAHSHUR AND SAQQARAH

Plate 82

*December 9–20, 1838*

After spending three days at Dendera, Roberts felt satisfied with the work he had done, and ordered the crew to set sail for Cairo; after the temples of ancient Egypt, the time had now come to look at Islamic architecture.
The nights had become very pleasant and the climate similar to the English weather towards the end of September, so the voyage promised to be very enjoyable. In the next few days Roberts spent much of his time finishing the drawings; when he counted them, he found that there were about a hundred. "Not bad for a month's work," he commented with legitimate pride. "Perhaps I did not do justice to these ancient relics, but few other artists in my circumstances could have afforded to stay longer, and I wonder how many of them could have produced more in the same time."
On the 10th he stopped for a few hours at Abydos, the main city sacred to Osiris, where he visited the few remains still visible of the temples of Seti I and Rameses II, which were to be excavated 21 years later by Auguste Mariette.
When he reached Siout on December 13, Roberts realized to his horror that he had left his portfolio of drawings on the heights of Girgeh, where he

had climbed two days earlier to compare some of his earlier sketches with the reliefs on the tombs in that area. As luck would have it, while he was wondering anxiously what to do, a southbound boat flying the Union Jack drew near, sailing before the wind.
On hearing of the incident the boat's owner offered to take Ismail and Hassan Amoris to Girgah to look for the drawings. Roberts was on tenterhooks until the 17th, when the pair returned triumphantly after covering the 80 miles between the two towns in only 30 hours, rowing nearly all the time in a hired rowing boat.
As if reborn after his anxious wait, Roberts decided to stop at Minieh to visit the bazaar. However, the weather was breaking and the days growing colder, so he decided to exploit the favorable wind in order to conclude the voyage as soon as possible. On the 20th the boat finally came in sight of the pyramids of Dahshur; the "Bent Pyramid" and the "Red Pyramid," both built by Snefru around 2570 BC, can be seen on the left-hand side of the lithograph, and the southern pyramids of the Saqqarah necropolis can be glimpsed on the horizon. In the foreground is a boat with a cargo of slave-girls, whose owner, an

unpleasant-looking Greek, began to sing the praises of with the skill of an auctioneer.
Disgusted, Roberts regretted that he only knew a few words of Arabic and Greek, not enough to express all his disapproval and the abhorrence with which the slave trade was regarded in England.

**From David Roberts's journal:**

*December 20 - This morning we came in sight of what are called the False Pyramids. The men sang all the time, happy at the thought that they will finally be home tonight. I have grown so used to their company that I am saddened at the thought of the imminent farewell. The journey has been fascinating, and undoubtedly the most important of my entire life. I believe that my drawings are of great interest, irrespective of their artistic worth.*

# CAIRO

*December 21, 1838 – February 6, 1839*

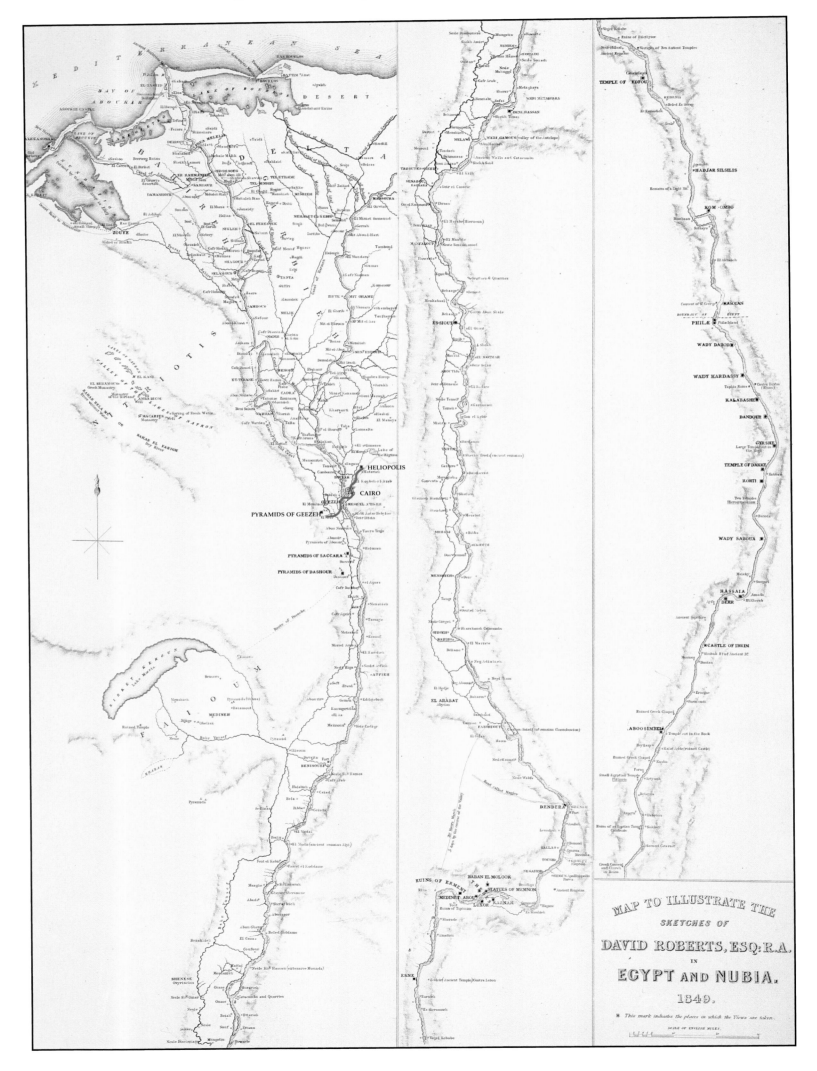

# EGYPT & NUBIA

FROM DRAWINGS MADE ON THE SPOT BY

David Roberts, R.A.

WITH HISTORICAL DESCRIPTIONS BY

WILLIAM BROCKEDON, F.R.S.

LITHOGRAPHED BY

LOUIS HAGHE.

David Roberts R.A.    L Haghe lith.

**From David Roberts's journal:**

*December 24 - From the heights of the Citadel, the spectacle offered at nightfall was magnificent. The sky was full of clouds, between which the rays of the setting sun managed to peep every so often; the pyramids loomed on the horizon, dark as the clouds that hung over them, and the Nile reflected the last glimmers of light, while the city stretched out as far as the eye could see, studded with fantastically shaped minarets. I am enjoying this Christmas Eve alone, grateful for being in good health and having concluded the most arduous part of the journey.*

# THE MOSQUE OF SULTAN HASSAN

<u>Plate 83</u>

*December 21–26, 1838*

When Roberts finally reached Cairo on the morning of December 21, he found a letter waiting for him from Christine, telling him of his election as an Associate of the Royal Academy. The next day he rented a house at a reasonable price and sent a letter to his daughter in which, together with his usual fatherly advice, he told her about his recent adventures and his plans for the immediate future. Above all he wished to add to his already bulky portfolio a comprehensive range of Cairo's mosques, which were unequaled throughout the world, although he was worried that the people might be hostile and almost certain that he would not be allowed to enter any of them. His only hope in this respect was Colonel Campbell, who was already making representations to the pasha. Roberts then spent a day or two writing more letters home and making his new residence as comfortable as possible. On the 23rd he made his first reconnaissance at the tombs of the Caliphs, and the next day visited the Citadel, then the magnificent residence of Mohammed Ali; he was given permission to visit the Audience Chamber and the pasha's private apartments, which he described as "all modern, and gaudily painted."

Roberts spent Christmas Day strolling around the city; after a walk through the city center he visited the Tombs of the Mamluks, followed by the great mausoleum recently built by Mohammed Ali, the reliefs of which seemed to him rather coarse compared with the delicacy of the older ones he had seen a little earlier. He was invited to lunch by Colonel Campbell, whose hospitality was as delightful as usual, and also spent a very pleasant evening.

The next morning he started work early. As his first subject he chose the majestic outline of the Mosque of Sultan Hassan, seen from the large square in front. While he was busy drawing, the guard provided for him by the pasha had difficulty keeping back the crowd of curious onlookers. The mosque is considered one of the greatest works of Islamic art; it was built by order of Sultan Hassan al-Nasir between 1356 and 1363, perhaps by a Syrian architect. The façades, featuring deep vertical niches containing two rows of windows, are surmounted by a projecting cornice made of stalactite work (muqarna) that was completed with crenellations at the turn of this century. The sultan's mausoleum, which projects from the building like a die, is surmounted by a 200-foot-tall dome rebuilt in the 18th century in a style influenced by Turkish art. The main minaret, 269 feet tall, is still the highest in Cairo.

# Victory Gate

Plate 84

*December 27, 1838*

On the morning of the 27th, Roberts made a drawing of Bab al-Nasr, the Victory Gate, one of the three surviving gates of those that opened in the city walls of Cairo built between 1087 and 1091 by the Vizier Badr el-Jamali. The mighty structure is flanked by two massive square towers, whose proportions were evidently inspired by the canons of ancient Roman *castrum* architecture. In the background, behind Bab al-Futuh (the Conquest Gate), stands the minaret of the mosque built between 990 and 1013 by the mysterious Caliph al-Hakim Bi Amrallah. In the afternoon Roberts went to Hill's Hotel, where he had stayed in September, to obtain news of England and exchange a few words with guests who had recently arrived from Europe. Later Colonel Campbell delivered the precious pass he would need during his imminent journey to the Holy Land. On his arrival in Cairo Roberts had made the acquaintance of two English gentlemen, John Pell and John Kinnear, who intended to travel to Syria after crossing the Sinai and Palestine. The pair invited him to join their expedition and the artist willingly agreed, particularly attracted by the idea of seeing the famous monastery of Saint Catherine. He immediately began the complex preparations for the journey, which seemed likely to be even more difficult than the one he had just finished.

# EL-RHAMREE MOSQUE

Plate 85

*December 27, 1838*

Near the Victory Gate stood El-Rhamree Mosque, whose elegant masonry with alternating rows of red and white stone betrayed its Mamluk origin; in other words, it dated from the period between 1250 and the incorporation of Egypt into the Ottoman Empire in 1517.

The Mamluks were originally bought slaves (mamluk in Arabic) of Turkish and Circassian descent who were trained as bodyguards or elite soldiers. This militia became increasingly powerful and overthrew the Ayubbid dynasty in a coup d'état. The regime of military feudalism they imposed was often bloodthirsty, but brought a period of economic, political and artistic glory to Egypt, largely due to the energetic personalities of sultans like Baybars, Hassan and Qalawun. Their last sovereign, Tuman Bey, was deposed by the Ottoman conquerors, but the Mamluks retained much of their power, often in open conflict with the pashas of Constantinople. During Napoleon's expedition to Egypt they offered strong resistance to the French troops, but were defeated at the Battle of the Pyramids, and their chiefs were treacherously massacred by Mohammed Ali, as they had become an obstacle to his desire for power.

In Mamluk architecture, the ornamental emphasis mainly focuses on the entrances, decorated with elaborate engravings and inlays in geometrical and floral patterns in accordance with the precept in the Koran that prohibits the portrayal of human beings or animals, and on the minarets, whose balconies are usually supported by a myriad of muqarnas. The domes, surmounted by the alam, the crescent-shaped metal ornament common to all styles of Islamic architecture, are usually so slender as to appear almost diaphanous. Although the monument was not particularly important, Roberts must have particularly liked the subject, as in both the lithograph and the watercolor displayed in Nottingham Museum the attention given to reproducing the contrast between the mysterious darkness of the alley and the soaring silhouette of the minaret is clearly evident.

David Roberts R.A.
L. Haghe. Lith.

The Minaret of the Mosque El Rhamree

# THE ZUWAILAH GATE
## FROM THE OUTSIDE

Plate 86

*December 28, 1838*

*R*oberts spent much of the 28th drawing Bab Zuwailah, one of the three monumental gates that still open in the remains of the ancient Fatimid city walls. The massive structure, formed by two semicircular towers that frame the single-arch portal, was completed around 1091. The great lobed blind arches that decorate its sides were a characteristic feature of North African architecture, imported to Egypt by craftsmen in the retinue of the Fatimid conquerors who ruled the country between 969 and 1171. The Fatimids, who came from what is now Tunisia, took their name from the family of Mohammed's daughter Fatima, whose descendants they claimed to be. Despite these decorative elements the gate, like Bab al-Nasr and Bab al-Futuh, clearly reveals the influence of the Roman-Byzantine construction style. The loggia on the portal, which was bricked up when Roberts saw it and has been reopened recently, originally housed the ceremonial orchestra, whose task was to announce the arrival of the royal court with music, in accordance with a protocol that is fairly common in the East. The gate is named after a brave North African tribe whose men fought in the Fatimid army.

David Roberts, R.A. I. Haghe, lith.                    Gate of the Metwalleys Cairo.

# The Zuwailah Gate
## FROM THE INSIDE

Plate 87

*December 28, 1838*

O n the two mighty towers of Bab Zuwailah stand the slender minarets of the al-Muayyad mosque, one of the most magnificent dating from the Circassian Mamluk age. The mosque, also called el-Ahmar (the Red), was begun in 1416 by Sultan al-Muayyad and completed a year after his death, in 1421.

*After its defensive function became unnecessary, Bab Zuwailah was long used as a prison, and sentences of capital punishment were carried out nearby. The mosque built onto the gate is the result of a curious political incident; al-Muayyad made a vow to build a sanctuary on the site of the prison into that he was thrown after a palace revolt, an incident that was by no means unusual in those days.*

*On regaining his freedom and his power, the sultan kept his vow. The bronze-clad doors of the entrance come from the Mosque of Sultan Hassan, and are considered some of the loveliest in Cairo; the interior, with its profusion of colored marble, stucco and gilding,*

*is extraordinarily but not exaggeratedly luxurious. The lithograph shows a view of the street that led from the gate to the city center; thronged with incessant traffic and lined with shops of all kinds on both sides, it was the scene of indescribable bedlam. Roberts, almost buried by the human tide, had to manage as best he could, as he was resigned to doing since his first few days in the city. Though picturesque, the narrow, crowded streets of Cairo constituted a rather difficult subject, because pedestrians continually ran the risk of being crushed by overloaded camels, which also had the unfortunate habit of shoving to the left and right with no respect for artists. The streets around Bab Zuwailah are still very busy and retain the atmosphere of bygone days, especially because of the numerous workshops specializing in the manufacture of the great canopies used to shade the streets during major ceremonies.*

**From David Roberts's journal:**

*December 28 - Today I made two drawings of the Bab Zuweileh gate with its minarets.*
*I am still bewildered by the extraordinarily picturesque appearance of the streets and buildings of this most wonderful of cities. Only the population is even more extraordinary, but a reliable description is impossible, and I will not even attempt one.*

Minarets and Grand Entrance
of the Metwaley at Cairo

# THE MARISTAN OF SULTAN QALAWUN

Plate 88

*December 29, 1838*

**From David Roberts's journal:**

*December 29 - The subjects are splendid, but very hard to draw in these narrow, crowded streets, although the passers-by usually behave very well towards me.*

*This view of the road leading to the Mosque of Sultan Qalawun shows the chaotic traffic that was one of the characteristic features of the city. For an artist dressed in the European style it was impossible to pass unnoticed, and discomfort sometimes gave way to a slight feeling of fear, though Roberts never suffered any serious incident. Although their curiosity was aroused by his appearance the people behaved very politely towards him; they usually did no more than gaze in amazement at his stock of pencils, paper and paints.*

*Nevertheless, in a letter to his friend David Hay, the artist had to admit that his irritation was sometimes hard to control. However, Cairo had some 300,000 inhabitants, a sixth more than Edinburgh, and it was unreasonable to expect to be able to wander around freely with no inconvenience, drawing undisturbed as if in the grounds of a Scottish castle. The complex, built in 1285 by Sultan al-Mansur Qalawun and consisting of a* madrasa, *the sultan's mausoleum and a hospital, is one of the most magnificent monuments*

*in Cairo. The most interesting and in many ways innovatory feature of this group of buildings (to which a* madrasa *was added by the sultan's son in the late 13th century) is certainly the hospital. It was not the first to be built in Cairo, as Ibn Tulun had already founded a similar charitable institution in the 9th century, imitated by the Fatimid sultans and by the great Saladin, but it was the best known, as it retained its function as a shelter for the sick and a center for the study of medicine until the 19th century. The sultan built the hospital on the basis of personal experience, as he had been successfully treated at the hospital of Nur al-Din in Damascus years earlier. The hospital, called* maristan *(place of illness), was far ahead of its time, as was Arab medical science, which was still taught in Europe at the beginning of the last century. The hospital was divided into two sections, for male and female patients, and received needy patients of all ages and social classes from all over the Arab world; a bed, food and appropriate treatment was guaranteed for all.*

# THE TOMBS OF MAMLUKS

Plate 89

*December 30, 1838*

**B**y contrast with the pharaonic custom of locating necropolises on the west bank of the Nile, the Mamluks built their sepulchres to the east, not far from the Citadel. Roberts visited the site on the 30th, a clear but very cold day. The huge depression contained a succession of minarets and domes of all shapes and sizes, even then in a dilapidated state; these monumental buildings housed the tombs of sultans, princesses and court dignitaries who lived during the great age of the Bahrite Mamluks and the Circassian Mamluks, between the 13th and 15th centuries. In time, a large number of smaller tombs were erected around the monumental buildings.
As it was the custom to go there to honor the dead on Fridays, closed courtyards and roofed areas were added to the tombs of the wealthier citizens for the use of visiting relatives, with the result that the cemeteries came to resemble towns. Nowadays, some 600,000 Cairo residents live in the huge necropolises outside the walls of the Fatimid city.
The tentacular capital city, which has grown beyond all recognition in the past few decades, has around 15 million inhabitants, many of whom live in dreadful conditions; it is therefore easy to understand the choice of those who prefer the vaguely supernatural peace of the city of the dead to the chaos of the new districts or the slums of the shanty towns.

# THE TOMBS OF MAMLUKS,
## WITH A FUNERAL PROCESSION

Plate 90

*December 30, 1838*

*The building reproduced by Roberts, which stands in the cemetery to the south of the Citadel, is known as the Sultan's Mausoleum. However, this name only indicates that it belonged to a person of high rank, as the mysterious monument has not yet been attributed, and is roughly dated at around 1360.*

*The main structure, which has a rectangular plan, is surmounted by twin fluted domes resting on very tall drums and connected by a barrel-vaulted* iwan; *a few yards away, situated in a corner of the enclosure wall that has now been destroyed, stands a soaring octagonal minaret that was probably part of the complex. The construction style of the mausoleum is out of the ordinary in many respects and presents some unusual analogies with the Central Asian architecture of Samarkand. The minaret that stands on the left of the building is part of the funerary complex of Emir Qusun, while the one silhouetted in the background dates from the Ottoman period. While Roberts was busy drawing, he suddenly heard loud shouts and laments. A few moments later he saw a funeral procession approaching, followed by veiled women weeping piteously; judging by the small size of the coffin, it must have been a child's funeral. The Scotsman was sincerely moved by this tragic scene, and included it in his view.*

# THE COPPERSMITHS' BAZAAR

Plate 91

*December 31, 1838*

airo's bazaars were too fascinating a subject for Roberts to resist, so on New Year's Eve he decided to visit the great market, which he portrayed in this magnificent view. With its colors and the groups of purchasers who lingered around one merchant or another to examine goods or haggle at length over prices, the bazaar provided an exciting spectacle, quite new to European eyes. Where the ancient city of the Fatimid dynasty once stood, the streets were now cluttered with goods of every kind. Scale makers vied for the little available space with fabric sellers, whose caverns were jam-packed with rolls of brightly colored silk and cotton. Not far away was a small jewelers' shop where jewelery could be valued or the price of some trinket bargained over. Each neighborhood specialized in a different type of goods; in one, perfumes and essences were sold, in another, spices and tea, and around the corner, carpets and haberdashery. Near the ancient religious complex of Sultan al-Salih Najm al-Din Ayyub, dating from 1243, coppersmiths and cauldron makers displayed embossed plates, bowls and cauldrons. In the midst of this bedlam pedestrians continually had to dodge carts laden with fruit, and freshwater sellers who staggered under the weight of the great jars they carried on their shoulders. Now as then, in the districts between the Citadel and Bab al-Futuh, craftsmen and shopkeepers with their baskets full of all sorts of products keep alive a tradition that seems eternal.

Drawing in the great bazaar involved no problems, but Roberts had a very different experience in a market in one of the poor districts of Cairo. While he was working with some difficulty in the midst of a curious crowd that continually interrupted him and even bumped into him by standing too close, he suddenly had his sketch pad torn out of his hands by a missile that appeared out of nowhere. It was a half-eaten orange, thrown from one of the galleries jutting out over the square, which must have been designed for that very purpose. Roberts decided that a change of scenery might be the wisest course of action but, irritated and perhaps rather ashamed of his inglorious retreat, he wondered whether an Arab artist would have taken to his heels quite as fast as he did.

The time had really come to wear more suitable clothing.

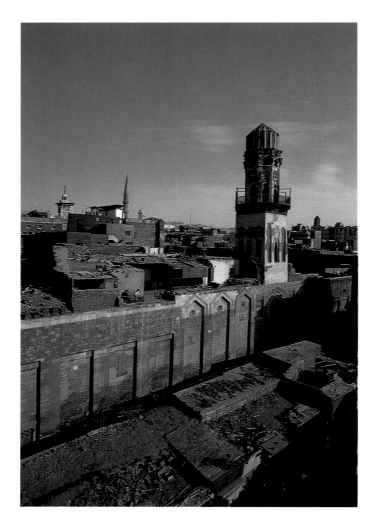

**From David Roberts's journal:**

*December 31 - It's New Year's Eve, but how different from those spent in London. The days are so bright, and I can eat fresh vegetables in abundance. I am in excellent health, and living in a city which surpasses the fantasy of any artist. I received a letter from my dearest Christine today; thank God all are well at home... This is the last night of the old year, and my thoughts turn to all the happy New Years I have spent so far. I send my heartfelt good wishes to all my nearest and dearest in my beloved Scotland.*

# The entrance to the Mosque of Sultan Hassan

Plate 92

*January 1, 1839*

On New Year's Day, Roberts was busy as usual in the streets of Cairo, looking for more picturesque subjects. Drawing in the midst of such a crowd was very tiring, so that by the time he got home in the evening he was worn out.
As he wrote in his journal, no-one in England, seeing those sketches, could possibly imagine how much labor they had cost him. In any event, his work would increase knowledge of the various architectural styles that had developed in Egypt over the centuries, and this was sufficient reward to justify all the effort he had put into it.
He spent that day drawing the magnificent entrance to the Mosque of Sultan Hassan, considered by many to be the loveliest in the whole of Cairo, although it was never completed.
The great structure was designed as a madrasa dedicated to the four orthodox law schools of Sunnite Islam (Maliki, Shafii, Hanbali and Hanafi), and also as a congregational mosque for the Friday sermon.
In the Islamic world, a madrasa was an institute in which students could study the legal/religious sciences, theology, grammar, literature and rhetoric free of charge. Founded towards the mid-11th century to strengthen Sunnite orthodoxy and combat Shiite propaganda, the madrasas are

far less widely attended now than they once were, but still combine the functions of mosque and theological seminary.
Sultan Hassan had the magnificent building erected in one of the most privileged positions in Cairo and lavished huge resources on it; however, near bankrupted by the increasing costs, he admitted that he would have abandoned the project if he had not been ashamed at the thought that someone might say an Egyptian sultan was incapable of finishing the mosque he had started. His death as a result of a court conspiracy put an end to all but part of his ambitious project.

# THE SCRIBE

Plate 93

*January 2–5, 1839*

On January 2, Roberts received a visit from the vice-consul, Mr. Walne, who told him what he needed to do to in order to obtain permission to enter the mosques. First of all, he would have to obtain suitable clothes, and secondly he would have to shave off his rather flashy sideburns. While the idea of dressing Turkish-style appealed to him, he was very sorry to lose the facial ornaments he was so proud of, but realized the concession was worth it. After all, he was the first European to be given such an opportunity, and there was no point worrying about such silly little details. Finally, he had to promise that he would not use brushes made of pig's bristles, as the pig is considered impure in the Islamic world. He spent the same day making the necessary purchases, although he did not feel quite well. As he strolled around the maze of alleys he was amazed at everything he saw: superb relics of a legendary past, extraordinary people and customs, indescribable lights and colors.

Cairo was so picturesque thàt it seemed to him to have no equal anywhere in the world. The only drawback was the evident poverty of much of the population, which particularly upset him. Among the many scenes of everyday life, he was particularly struck by the sight of a young woman, evidently illiterate, who was dictating a letter to a public scribe with a sorrowful expression; this lithograph betrays the human compassion Roberts felt for those poor people.

When he got home he tried on the new clothes and was pleased with the result; with his now sunburned skin and dark eyes he could reasonably pass for a Turk. He had not shaved his head, but his hair was well concealed under the turban, and to complete the effect he would grow a mustache in accordance with the local fashion.

Despite his enthusiasm, he had to delay the long-awaited experience for a few days because an unpleasant gastrointestinal disorder confined him to bed until the 5th, when he was able to take a walk through the town to regain his strength.

**From David Roberts's journal:**

*January 4 - Having heard from my servant of my indisposition, Colonel Campbell came to see me, and I spent a very pleasant hour with him. Later I wrote a long letter to my friend Hay, and spent the rest of the time profitably, retouching the drawings I had done in the past few days.*

# THE SILK VENDORS' BAZAAR AND THE RELIGIOUS COMPLEX OF SULTAN AL-GHURI

<u>Plate 94</u>

*January 6, 1839*

On January 6, Roberts, now entirely recovered, finally went out dressed "Turkish-style," ready to visit the interior of as many mosques as possible. Escorted by two armed guards, he went (among other places) to al-Azhar Mosque, the most important architectural relic to survive in Cairo from the Fatimid period. Built in 972 by Vizier Jawhar al-Siqilli and once used, at least in part, as a theological college, it was rebuilt in an even more impressive form after the earthquake of 1303. During Ottoman rule, when the Mamluk madrasas had fallen into decline, al-Azhar became the center of Islamic teaching in Egypt, and it is still the most famous religious university in the Arab world. Although its name means "The Splendid," Roberts felt that it was in an appallingly dilapidated condition, and did not even draw it.

He received a better impression from Saiydna al-Hussein Mosque, rebuilt in 1792 on the site of a much older place of worship; as the head of Mohammed's nephew Hussein, who died in the Battle of Kerbela in 680, is buried there, the sanctuary is still considered one of the most sacred, and is magnificently decorated during Ramadan, the month of fasting. The same day he also entered the funerary mosque of Sultan Qaytbay, dating from 1474, where he was shown an exquisitely illuminated copy of the Koran. During his visit to the bazaar quarter, Roberts was particularly struck by a section of the street between two sacred buildings over which wooden boards had been erected to offer shade to the silk merchants, and decided to return there. Apart from that makeshift roof, this part of the city has remained almost unchanged. The madrasa and the mausoleum built circa 1504 by Sultan al-Ghuri still stand opposite one another on al-Muizz Street.

Both buildings have a trefoil stalactite work portal in the façade, and alternate rows of white, red and black stone. Numerous shops and kiosks still do a roaring trade along the street, and the rent they pay to occupy public property is used for the maintenance of the complex.

David Roberts R.A. London 1849 Bazaar of the Silk Mercers, Cairo

**From David Roberts's journal:**

*January 6 - It makes my hair stand on end to think what terrifying punishment would have been inflicted on me for my involuntary crime if it had become known that the sacred drapery had been contaminated by the touch of an infidel, a Christian dog, and I had been caught.*

# THE INTERIOR OF THE MOSQUE OF SULTAN AL-GHURI

Plate 95

*January 6, 1839*

Roberts was able to enter and draw the interior of the madrasa-mosque of Sultan al-Ghuri, richly decorated with colored marble. This lithograph is of particular interest because it shows the appearance of a mosque built on the qa'a plan, the same one used by Sultan Hassan to build his masterpiece. Very briefly, an atrium with some degree of decoration leads to an unroofed square courtyard, which may have a fountain for ritual ablutions in the middle; four prayer rooms (iwans) with vaulted or coffered ceilings surround this courtyard. The main iwan, in the end wall of which is the mihrab or prayer niche, is larger than the other three. This cross-shaped plan is typical of the madrasas-mosques built during the 13th century, in which the rooms used for study and the students' lodgings are usually built around the iwans to form a square. The rooms were lit by countless oil lamps and great bronze chandeliers similar to the one portrayed by Roberts; the few surviving specimens are now mostly housed in the Cairo Museum of Islamic Art. Dressed as a high-ranking army officer, the artist visited the mosque accompanied by two guards, who waited at the door, and one of the pasha's young officials who had been educated in England. This official's quick thinking proved providential when Roberts got into a scrape that could have had very serious results. Entrance to a mosque for a non-Muslim was strictly prohibited and subject to very heavy penalties; Mohammed Ali had granted permission to Roberts provided that he dress and act in such a way that he would not be recognized as a Christian. However, overcome by curiosity, after a while the Scotsman entered a room where a number of people where working on a large silk cloth with magnificent gold embroidery. He knelt down as he had seen other onlookers do, not to kiss the fabric but to examine it more closely. The menacing silence that suddenly fell was enough to make him realize that he had done something terrible; when he looked up, he saw his young escort put a finger to his lips and then draw it across his throat. With a glimmer of good sense he prostrated himself again and began to move backwards, while the official covered his retreat. Once outside the mosque he took to his heels and ran through a couple of districts. Later, he was told that the cloth was the sacred drape woven specially for pilgrims to lay on the tomb of the Prophet at Medina.

In Entrance to the Citadel of Cairo.

# The Citadel Gate

Plate 96

*January 7–8, 1839*

On January 7 Roberts climbed the heights of Moqattam to see the famous petrified forest. The next day his attention was attracted by the preparations taking place in the square in front of Bab el-Asab, the main entrance to the Citadel. Here, caravans bound for Mecca were being prepared, and crowds of pilgrims were flocking from all over the city and the surrounding area. One of the camels was to take to Medina the precious cloth that was to be placed on the Prophet's tomb. As far as the eye could see, the windows and even the roofs of the houses were packed with onlookers, mainly women and children, watching the spectacle with great excitement.

Now, the great square Midan Salah el-Din has lost its original function, but has remained one of the nerve centers of the great metropolis. It is overlooked by the Mosque of Pasha Mahmud and the adjacent madrasa, Qani bey Amir Akor, shown in the lithograph on the right-hand side of the Citadel Gate. Opposite Bab el-Asab stands the great Mosque of Sultan Hassan, with al-Rifai Mosque facing it. Completed in 1912 by order of Princess Khoshiar Hanem, it contains (among others) the tombs of King Farouk, last sovereign of Egypt, and the Shah of Persia Reza Pahlavi.

The Citadel of Cairo, Residence of Mehemet Ali

David Roberts, R.A.    L. Haghe, lith.

# THE DEPARTURE OF PILGRIMS BOUND FOR MECCA

Plate 97

*January 8, 1839*

**From David Roberts's journal:**

*8 January - Today I made some sketches of the departure ceremony of the caravan which will take the sacred cloth to be placed on the Prophet's tomb. This evening I dined with friends in accordance with the local customs, in other words sitting on cushions around a very low table, and using my fingers to pick up meat cut into small pieces.*

Roberts also drew the departure of the caravan bound for Medina and Mecca. In the lithograph, the pilgrims are leaving the city in the direction of Suez; the huge bulk of the Citadel is silhouetted in the background. The great fortress, which stands on a rocky eminence on the slopes of Jebel Moqattam, where it overlooks the city, was built in 1176 by Saladin; part of the outer layer of the minor pyramids of Giza may have been used as building material. The building was extended several times over the centuries; inside its mighty enclosure wall Mohammed Ali erected a magnificent residence, now used as a museum. The same sovereign started work on a great mosque in Ottoman style in 1824, which was far from complete when Roberts saw it; in fact, the Alabaster Mosque was only finished by his son Said in 1857. The pasha is said to have built it to redeem his soul, tormented by a horrific crime. Mohammed Ali, who was of Albanian descent but born in Greece, went to Egypt with Turkish troops to liberate the country from the Napoleonic occupation. His boundless ambition led him to proclaim himself pasha in 1805, and in 1811, wishing to get rid of the Mamluks, who constituted an obstacle to his political ambitions, he invited them to the Citadel on a pretext and had them slaughtered.

# THE INTERIOR OF THE MOSQUE OF SULTAN AL-MUAYYAD

Plate 98

*January 9, 1839*

*T*he religious complex built by Sultan al-Muayyad behind Bab Zuwailah included a mosque for Friday prayers, a madrasa and two mausoleums. Roberts visited it on the afternoon of January 9, after spending the morning painting studies in oils of the interior of the funerary mosque of Sultan Qaytbay.

The interior of the mosque, which was built between 1416 and 1421, is a huge hypostyle room divided into a nave and two aisles, supported by columns with Corinthian capitals of pre-Islamic manufacture, certainly reused. The coffered ceilings made of painted and gilded wood, the windows with their elegant stucco frames, the finely decorated wood and ivory pulpit and the dikka (the imam's dais), visible in the center of the lithograph, which rested on slender marble columns, make the mosque one of the loveliest in Cairo. It is a sad loss that only part of the complex has survived to the present day; in fact, the present mosque only occupies one of the four original iwans. At sunset Roberts hurried home so that he would have plenty of time to tidy up and change into sufficiently elegant clothes, as he had been invited to the inaugural performance at the city's opera house. The building was "small but tasteful" and he enjoyed the opera, sung in Italian.

Interior of the Mosque of the Metwalys

# A COFFEEHOUSE

Plate 99

*January 10, 1839*

**D**uring his long strolls through the city streets, Roberts was enraptured by the picturesque scenes of local life. In one spot old men dozed near a stall crammed with nameless goods, a little further on an interested crowd watched a juggler's performance, and just around the corner a shopkeeper was fighting a losing battle, sweeping into the street the dust that had just covered the worn shop floor.

Here and there, from some mysterious recess, came scents of spices and grilled meat that mingled with the aroma issuing from the countless coffeehouses, popular meeting places that were crowded at all hours of the day with an all-male clientele. Here, colorfully dressed men spent their time drawing on a long chabouk or bubbling shisha and lazily blowing out curls of blue smoke, lost in thought, or idly indulged in endless discussions around a cup of coffee prepared Turkish style and sipped slowly according to an ancient ritual. Fascinated and delighted by this exotic world, Roberts confided all his impressions to his faithful sketchpad.

David Roberts, R.A.                    L.Haghe, Lith.

# The Tombs
## of the Caliphs

Plate 100

*January 11, 1839*

*Tombs of the Caliph's Cairo.*

*D*uring the second half of the 13th century, huge monumental necropolises were built to the east of the Fatimid walls; as in the case of the burial grounds situated to the west of the Citadel, they have now been swallowed up by the continually expanding metropolis. Here too, the expanse of bulbous domes and minarets houses a large proportion of the poorer segment of the population, in strange coexistence between the living and the dead.

On January 11, Roberts drew some attractive views of what are still incorrectly called the Tombs of the Caliphs; in fact, the caliphate came to an end in 1258 with the death of the last Abbasid sovereign in Baghdad, while these mausoleums date from the great period of the two Mamluk dynasties. The title of caliph (which literally means "successor") was attributed to the successors of Mohammed, who acted as his deputies; these "princes of believers" and defenders of Islam held executive and legal power, governing as absolute rulers. The sultans, originally less important than the caliphs, acquired the role of monarchs with the advent of the Mamluks. The lithograph, which is pervaded by decadent romanticism yet does not indulge in pathos, constitutes an excellent example of the descriptive skills mastered by the Scottish artist.

231

# THE RUINS OF A MINARET NEAR THE CITADEL

Plate 101

*January 11, 1839*

As he strolled among the Tombs of the Caliphs, Roberts was particularly struck by a ruined minaret standing alone, surrounded by the weather-beaten remains of some other funerary mosques. An atmosphere of melancholy desolation hung over these mute witnesses of past grandeur. Engrossed, Roberts observed the extraordinary variety of forms and decorations surrounding him and the myriad of lines multiplied endlessly, no two of which were alike, in supreme contrast with the severe geometry of the Pyramids, towering on the horizon.

The oldest mosques had no minarets, and the muezzins issued their call to prayer from the rooftops. The first to be built in Cairo was the spiral minaret of the Mosque of Ibn Tulun, designed on the Mesopotamian pattern.

Tall, graceful buildings with a square plan, surmounted by a kiosk with a domed roof, began to appear in the 11th century. Increasingly complex designs developed from these early specimens, and their development passed through various stages, from a square to an octagonal, and later a round shape, and finally multistorey buildings in which the individual elements freely overlapped.

Slender, pencil-shaped minarets, usually with a single balcony, only became fashionable after 1517, following the Turkish conquest. As soon as it was imported into Egypt, Ottoman architecture assimilated some of the local building styles, including the use of two-color-striped masonry called ablaq, which had been imported to Egypt from Andalusia in the 14th century with great success. Whenever it was impossible to obtain different-colored building materials for financial reasons, the ablaq pattern was painted on the plaster.

**From David Roberts's journal:**

*January 11 - Today I sketched the Tombs of the Caliphs.
I have received a letter from my dear Christine who tells me that all at home are well, thank God.*

Ruined Mosques in the Desert, West of the Citadel.

David Roberts, R.A.

L. Haghe lith.

233

# THE INTERIOR OF THE MOSQUE OF SULTAN HASSAN

Plate 102

*January 12, 1839*

*A*lthough Sultan Hassan never completed his mosque, the harmony of the building and the elegant understatement of the decorations make it a masterpiece that has no equal in Egypt for grandeur and majesty. The building has an irregular pentagonal plan in which the cross-shaped structure of the madrasa is inserted. Inside is a square central courtyard adorned with the fountain shown here, and the four iwans (prayer rooms) with their high barrel vaults are distributed around this well of light. The play of light and shade, the purity of the lines and the huge volumes are highly conducive to prayer.

On January 12, while Roberts was drawing the inner courtyard of the mosque, a good-looking young man spoke to him, interested in his activity. His name was Hanafee Ismail Effendi and, to the artist's great surprise, not only did he speak excellent English, but he had also been baptized in Glasgow during one of his journeys. Brought up and educated in the European style, he was a member of the pasha's entourage. The two immediately struck up a friendship that was to have important future developments: Ismail accompanied Roberts on his journey to the Holy Land and kept in touch with him by letter for many years afterwards.

# THE SLAVE MARKET

Plate 103

*January 13–14, 1839*

Accompanied by some of his new friends, such as John Pell and Frenchman Linant de Bellefonds whom he had already met several months earlier in Alexandria, Roberts set off into the desert, a few miles from Cairo, at dawn on January 13. Here, the pilgrims bound for Mecca were preparing to strike camp and begin their long journey. There were "roughly 2,000 camels and at least two or three hundred horses." Surrounded by an incredible throng from all the Islamic tribes, among which those from Constantinople were particularly numerous, stood the emir's tent.

Confusion was rife, but the great crowd constituted an impressive sight. Wild-eyed, half-naked dervishes, their skin and even their lips transfixed by skewers and daggers, mingled with the other pilgrims. After the midday prayer a gunshot was fired, and at that signal the seething mass moved eastward amid a cacophony of sounds issuing from instruments of all shapes and sizes, which gave the caravan a joyful appearance quite foreign to what should have been a very solemn moment.

The scene reminded Roberts of the Biblical passage describing the journey of the children of Israel through the desert. Although he had brought his drawing materials with him, there was such chaos that he was unable to get much work done. However, the experience was an unforgettable one, and there was a great deal to talk about on the way back. Roberts spent the next day procuring the materials he needed for his imminent expedition to the Holy Land; he bought water bottles, blankets, some pistols, a saber and various other articles. Although he admired the beauty of Cairo, as he strolled in the maze of the bazaar and the streets of the city center he could not reconcile himself to the appalling poverty he saw all around him and the frequent scenes of tyranny against which his indignant spirit rebelled. He was always horrified by the sight of beggars lying in the middle of the road, young conscripts led to the barracks in chains, and hanged men dangling from a rope in the middle of the main square, exposed to public scorn as a terrible warning of the pasha's justice. What really made his blood boil, though, was the degrading spectacle of the slave market, a barbarous custom that shamed the whole country.

# A MOSQUE IN THE SUBURB OF BOULAK

Plate 104

*January 15, 1839*

*A*lthough his knowledge of the Islamic world was rather sketchy, Roberts paid great attention to the superb architecture of the mosques, which greatly appealed to his aesthetic sensibility.

He had already come into contact with Arab art during his journey to Spain years earlier, but the delicate colored masonry, the lightness of the stuccos and the carved stone lacework, and the purity of the lines that appeared before his dazzled gaze every day were absolutely unrivaled.

While he was strolling through the alleys of the port suburb of Boulak, which he visited on the morning of the 15th, this interest continued to predominate, so that in this lithograph the eye is drawn to the sanctuary in the background, right in the focal center of the composition.

Mosques, the most important architectural works in Islamic art, can be divided into three categories: the jami, *the mosque used for community prayers on Fridays; the* masjid, *the place of prayer and meditation, from which the modern word mosque is derived; and the* sawiya, *or commemorative chapel. As there were no major conflicts between the religious, dogmatic and social rules of Islam gradually defined by the four main schools already*

*mentioned, it was sometimes possible to hold different rites in the same building.*

*Another type of building was the* khanqa, *a sort of* madrasa-*monastery where those who preferred a mystic and esoteric approach to religious doctrines lived and studied, and where solitude and asceticism played*

*fundamental roles.*

*Mosques,* madrasas *and* khanqas *were often associated with the mausoleums of important people to form a single complex.*

*From Boulak, Roberts was ferried to the Isle of Rhoda, an oasis of greenery in the middle of the Nile.*

David Roberts R.A.

239

Tombs of the Khalifs
Cairo

David Roberts R.A.
Sketched

240

# THE MOSQUE OF SULTAN AL-ASHRAF QAYTBAY

Plate 105

*January 16, 1839*

*The surreal atmosphere emanating from the Mamluk necropolises evidently had a special appeal for the Scottish artist, as he returned to draw there on the 16th. One of the most famous of the Tombs of the Caliphs is that of Sultan al-Ashraf Qaytbay, consisting of various structural elements that culminate in the splendid funerary mosque; it was the custom of the sovereigns of that period to build a mosque or a* madrasa *next to their mausoleum. The underground funerary chamber in which the body was placed with its head wrapped in a white cloth, facing Mecca, was usually bare of ornament, while the domed room above it abounded in decoration.*

*Sultan Qaytbay, whose long reign marked the apogee of the Circassian Mamluk period, built himself a particularly magnificent tomb, featuring an architectural style that paid more attention to detail than to the gigantic structures of the past. The decorative taste of the period also brought a golden age in the carving of marble, which was widely used on façades too.*

*Built between 1472 and 1474, this monument is considered one of the greatest masterpieces of Mamluk architecture, in view of the sublime balance of its proportions and its wealth of ornament; the fine latticework covering the surface of the dome like lace, and the elegant shape of the 130-foot-tall minaret, are particularly exquisite. In the interior, the prayer room has a splendid mosaic floor made of with multicolored marble pieces. Alongside Sultan Qaytbay's mausoleum is a vestibule in which the tombs of his four wives were placed, bathed in the soft light that enters from the stained-glass windows.*

*The character of the sultan contrasts strangely with this delicate elegance; ambitious and obstinate, he extorted huge sums of money through crippling taxes to finance an expensive building program in the capital and an interminable battle against the Ottoman Empire, which only concluded with the peace treaty of 1491. Though an aesthete and a lover of the fine arts, he was sadly famous for his sudden, apparently uninstigated fits of terrible violence.*

# THE KHANQA OF
# SULTAN FARAJ IBN BARQUQ

Plate 106

*January 16, 1839*

When Roberts visited Cairo, many of the most glorious monuments of the past were in a sad state of neglect, and all memory of many had been lost. The artist also had little if any knowledge of the local language, which made it very difficult for him to obtain information about the magnificent buildings he took as his subjects. This explains the rather vague titles sometimes given to Haghe's lithographs. Although this one is simply described as "One of the Tombs of the Caliphs," it is actually the Khanqa of Sultan Faraj Ibn Barquq, one of the greatest masterpieces of Circassian Mamluk architecture.

Although he had already built a mausoleum inside the city walls, Sultan al-Zahir Barquq, founder of the Circassian dynasty, asked on his deathbed to be buried next to the tombs of the Sufis, in the cemetery to the east of the Fatimid city. In order to grant his request, his son al-Nasir Faraj built a great khanqa with two mausoleums, one for his father and the other for himself.

Even though he had been a brave warrior who repulsed the Ottomans and Tamerlane's Mongol hordes, al-Zahir was attracted by the ascetic-mystic practices of the Sufis, which explains his request. Sufism, though originally opposed by the orthodox schools of theology, became popular in the 11th century, and came to exercise considerable political and social influence over Islam, giving rise to the cult of the saints, religious brotherhoods, and Arabic-Persian poetry that speaks of divine love in the guise of amatory and Bacchic verses.

The khanqa, built between 1400 and 1411, is a huge structure with a square plan, with two minarets and a dome surmounting each mausoleum. The symmetry of the whole is almost perfect, and quite rare for the architecture of the period. The lithograph shows the north entrance of the building, and the nearby arched gallery supported by columns, called a sabil-kuttab.

The funerary complex was intended to include a camel market and other commercial buildings, which were never completed because of the premature death of al-Nasir, executed by his emirs on the instigation of Sheik al-Mahmudi, the future Sultan al-Muayyad. What might seem a strange mixture of functions was by no means unusual, as cemeteries were not considered to be the sole province of the dead. They even included residential blocks and mansions, where the wealthy resided on the occasion of festivals in honor of the dead and during their regular visits to the tombs of their loved ones.

# THE PYRAMIDS OF GIZA
## SEEN FROM THE NILE

Plate 107

*January 17, 1839*

On January 17, the day he returned to the Pyramids after his first visit on October 3, Roberts wrote in his journal, "I cannot express my feelings at the sight of these gigantic monuments." His emotional reaction is shared by all those who have ever stood in the shadow of these giants, with their geometrically perfect lines. Since ancient times the great tombs of the pharaohs of the 4th dynasty (2570–2450 BC) have inspired a huge amount of literature, pyramidology have emerged. Now that the burial function of the pyramids has been established, modern archaeologists are not very interested in imaginative speculation, but are endeavoring to discover the engineering techniques that enabled the builders to overcome physical and organizational problems that are difficult to solve even today. Roberts drew this view from the east bank of the Nile, near the landing stage of the Giza ferry. From there,

full of hypotheses about their construction, the mysterious significance of their proportions, and the esoteric secret of the orientation on the basis of which they were aligned on the low plateau of the Libyan desert. The travelers of the past began to wonder what their purpose was, while in more recent times, self-styled pioneers of the new and fascinating, though dubious, science of the pyramids appear to be arranged in order of size: from right to left can be seen the pyramid of Cheops, then the pyramid of Chephren (which appears to be the tallest because it is built on a rise in the ground), and finally the pyramid of Mykerinus, followed by the minor pyramid of a queen, the proportions of which were exaggerated by the artist. Until the 19th century, travelers could only reach the area of the Pyramids without too much difficulty when the Nile was low and the surrounding canals empty; it took just over an hour to travel from Cairo to Madiah, cross the river by boat and reach the village of Giza.

The journey became much longer and more complicated during the floods, when the area turned into a swamp.

# THE PYRAMIDS OF CHEOPS AND CHEPHREN

Plate 108

*January 17, 1839*

**G**reek historian Herodotus, who visited Egypt in 450 BC, tried to find an answer to the numerous questions posed by the Pyramids and their construction. In his second book, Histories, he tells how the Great Pyramid was built. According to his account, 100,000 men, working in three-month shifts, first built a succession of steps, hauling the stones with the aid of wooden machines, and then covered the structure with well-polished blocks of stone. Cheops is described as a tyrant who imposed on his people "ten years' hardship spent on this mammoth task."

Similar comments were made by another historian, Diodorus Siculus, who lived four centuries later. In fact, neither of the two accounts is true; it has now been established that the workforce, consisting of 50,000 men, was recruited for only three-and-a-half months a year, at the time of the floods, over a period of 22 years. Peasants and young men from all walks of life constituted the backbone of the seasonal army that worked on the building site for the pharaoh, whose divine nature justified the huge size of the tomb and the effort required to build it.

According to current theory, accusations of slavery are unjustified, because the workmen volunteered their labor in return for the deceased's intercession with the sun god Ra. Like the people of medieval Europe who expiated their sins by building great cathedrals, the ancient Egyptians agreed to be divided into squads and supervised by government-employed engineers in order to acquire merit with the gods.

The techniques used to build these extraordinary monuments are not yet known – perhaps overlapping ramps, raised as the work progressed – but the statistics are astonishing. The pyramid of Cheops occupies a larger volume than any other building erected in ancient times (over 3,000,000 cubic feet), and its original height of 485 feet was unequaled until the construction of the bell towers of the Gothic cathedral in Cologne, four thousand years later.

# THE SPHINX

Plate 109

*January 17, 1839*

The Sphinx, which is aptly called Abu el-Hol (Father of Terror) in Arabic, stands in the desert sands in front of the east side of the pyramid of Chephren.
The reclining statue is 66 feet tall, and some 188 feet long. The great effigy with the body of a lion was carved from a spur of limestone rock originally used for quarrying, while the paws and tail were made with added blocks.

As shown in the lithograph, for a long time the face was the only part of the statue to emerge from the sand; some 16 feet tall, it still presents traces of color, which were more evident when Roberts saw it than they are now.

At the time of Herodotus, the great monument must actually have been invisible, as the historian makes no mention of it. The colossus had the features of the Pharaoh Chephren, portrayed as the living image of the sun god, guardian of the necropolis of Giza. From the time of the New Kingdom, the Sphinx was identified with the god Harmakhis ("Horus on the horizon") or even, with daring syncretism, with a deity that incorporated the triple form of the sun during its journey through the sky: Khepri at dawn, Ra in the splendor of midday, and Atum at sunset.

The Sphinx has been damaged on various occasions, the last time by musket shots fired by Mamluk soldiers, and has undergone numerous restorations at various periods. The most famous one was ordered by Thutmoses IV, to whom Harmakhis himself appeared in a dream, calling for the statue to be unearthed and restored to its ancient splendor.

A granite stele commemorating the event is still visible between the front paws.

# THE SPHINX
## SEEN FROM THE FRONT

Plate 110

*January 17, 1839*

*S*phinxes *(the Greek name "sphinx" derives from the Egyptian* shesep ankh, *or "living image"), which were very common throughout ancient Egypt, were effigies of the pharaoh or a protecting deity. In archaic times the sovereign had been compared with a lion and portrayed as one, but it was not until the 4th dynasty that sculptors gave the beast a human head, usually adorned by the characteristic royal headgear called the* nemes, *and the* uraeus. *Especially in Thebes, sphinxes sometimes had the head of a ram, an animal sacred to Amun-Ra, or a falcon, the symbol of Horus.*
*The most famous of these statues is the great Sphinx of Giza, a monument that has become the emblem of ancient Egyptian civilization. Buried by the sands of the Libyan desert, the colossus was excavated in 1798 by scientists accompanying Napoleon's expedition, and 18 years later, by Italian Giovanni Caviglia, who also found some scattered fragments of the statue, now in the British Museum.*
*The restoration work that gave the Sphinx its present appearance was performed between 1925 and 1936 by Egyptologists Emile Baraize and Selim Hassan. Note the obviously incorrect date on the picture; the drawing for this lithograph was certainly not made on July 17, 1839, when Roberts was already back in England, but, more accurately, six months earlier.*

# The arrival of the simùn in Giza

Plate 111

*January 17, 1839*

oberts very probably made the preparatory drawing for this famous lithograph when he got back home. The composition is a sort of tribute to the mysterious, exotic charm of ancient Egypt in general and the Sphinx in particular, and constitutes one of the few exceptions to the artist's strict rule of portraying a real situation. While the sky is blazing with the last rays of the setting sun, a violent sandstorm is about to overtake the caravan camped at the foot of the Sphinx, whose eternally enigmatic smile seems to express imperturbable indifference to the imminent fury of the wind.

The sky is heavy with sand pushed forward in thicker and thicker waves, and the men are seeking shelter from the fury of the simùn. The moment is fraught with dramatic tension: The enigmatic force emanating from the gigantic face and the mystery of the looming pyramids are actually tangible, yet all is unreal, a magnificent fiction produced by the excited sensibilities of Roberts,

who drew on his imagination and fully exploited the poetic license granted to him.

In reality, the Sphinx faces the rising sun, whereas here it faces west and the sun is setting to the south; the pyramid of Mykerinus is too close, and those of the queens are faraway on the horizon, as if separated from their lord and master.

The simùn, a hot, dry wind that rages with indescribable violence for a few minutes, usually blows from the desert in spring, and it is very unlikely that Roberts witnessed a scene like the one portrayed here. Nevertheless, this view is one of the most dramatic in the entire collection, and is certainly among those with the greatest emotional impact.

In January 1850, Roberts gave his friend Charles Dickens a small oil painting of a similar subject. To those who pointed out these anomalies, the great author replied that artists are allowed to take poetic license.

# VIEW OF CAIRO
## LOOKING WESTWARD

Plate 112

*January 18, 1839*

*R*oberts devoted the whole of the 18th to seeking the best viewpoints from which to draw some general views of the city. Cairo was already a chaotic, complex metropolis in which buildings dating from different periods were jumbled together with no apparent order. The only explanation for such chaos is a history full of radical changes and dramatic events. The first settlement, which the Greeks called Babilonia, stood on the site where the fatal battle between the benevolent god Horus and the treacherous god Seth is supposed to have taken place in ancient times. The capital of Egypt was then Memphis, and later moved to Thebes. After the conquest of Egypt by Alexander the Great in 332 BC, royal power was transferred to the recently founded Alexandria, which maintained its primacy under Roman rule and during the rapid spread of Christianity. In 639 Babilonia was conquered by Amr Ibn al-As, the Arab general who introduced Islam into the country; two years later, Caliph Omar Ibn al-Khalab decided to found a new capital, which he called al-Fostat, near the ancient Byzantine fortress. In 750 the Abbasid dynasty deposed the Omayyads and began the construction of the city of al-Askar, a military capital that soon expanded and merged with al-Fostat to form a huge

metropolis. One hundred twenty years later, Ahmed Ibn Tulun founded a third fortified capital, which absorbed the previous two cities within a few decades. The true foundation of Cairo, by Fatimid General Gobar al-Sikkili, dates from 969, however; the city then took the name of al-Qahira (The Victorious), and a long

period began during which the urban area spread north and east as far as the slopes of Mount Moqattam. The reign of Saladin, which began in 1176, initiated a new era in the history of Cairo; during his rule the city walls were extended and the Citadel was built. The Mamluk era also brought with it a major period

of urbanization, which was enthusiastically continued by the Ottoman rulers when Egypt became a province of the Turkish Empire. The development that brought Cairo to its present stage began in 1805, under Pasha Mohammed Ali, after the brief Napoleonic occupation.

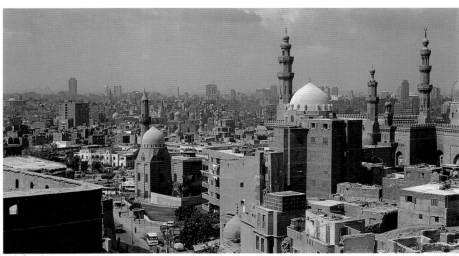

255

**From David Roberts's journal:**

*January 18 - Today I received a letter from my dear friend Durrant, from whom I heard that my dear Christine is well.*

# VIEW OF CAIRO
## LOOKING EASTWARD

Plate 113

*January 18, 1839*

The city is portrayed looking east, from the point where the crowded district of el-Saiyda Zeinab now lies; the huge bulk of the Mosque of Sultan Hassan can be seen on the left, the Citadel on the right, and the Citzenib Gate in the foreground. From the surrounding heights, the immense conurbation looked like an ocean of earth-colored houses, permanently veiled by a patina of fine desert sand carried on the wind. The sight was made even more astonishing by the slender silhouettes of hundreds of minarets soaring towards the sky. Roberts was fascinated yet dismayed at the sight of a world so incomparably distant and different from his own. In Cairo the most extreme contrasts could be seen every day: Coptic Arabs, Bedouins, Turks, Berbers and fellahin formed an indescribable mixture ceaselessly flowing along the streets, while in the silent mosques, white-gowned muezzins leafed through the pages of the Koran. In the meandering streets of the city, relics of a legendary past mingled with everyday poverty, and elegant architecture clashed violently with the barbaric sight of slaves taken to market.

# THE FAÇADE OF A HOUSE

Plate 114

*January 19, 1839*

*I*ncreasingly fascinated by Islamic architecture, Roberts devoted a whole day, the 19th, to studying the typical construction and decoration techniques used in Cairo. First he visited a number of houses, including an old mansion that must have been magnificent in its day, but had been soarly neglected. He described this condition as being sadly common to much of that unfortunate country, which had fallen into decay after a long period of maladministration and continual wars. After lunch, he went to the main city square, where the pasha had opened several building sites. The stone blocks and the bowls used to prepare the mortar were carried on the shoulders of numerous young women, supervised by a guard who meted out rather generous lashes of his whip with equanimity. The scene was accompanied by a continual buzz of noise, to which only the superintendents, sitting cross-legged in front of their inseparable chabouks, seemed to be oblivious.

The start of Islamic architecture in Cairo dates from the 9th century, with the construction of the Mosque of Ibn Tulun and the Nilometer on the Isle of Rhoda, although they betray an evident Mesopotamian influence. Only with the advent of the Fatimids did an independent style begin to develop, with a clear preference for highly complex decorations in which arabesques in geometrical frames and the entwined star motif predominate. The influence of Syrian art was mainly evident during Ayyubid rule and the first Mamluk period; among other things, stucco ornaments, the use of stained glass, masonry with bands of alternating colors, and stalactite-work pendentives (which from then on became a characteristic feature of Egyptian architecture) were introduced. The Circassian Mamluks preferred marble facing, and took the technique of building great domes to the height of perfection. Apart from a few exceptions, Turkish rule marked the decline of monumental building activities and led to a general regression in decorative taste.

However, it was European interference that struck the final blow at the creativity of local architecture, which became very similar to that of the great western cities. Most private homes, unlike the mosques, were sadly demolished starting in the mid-19th century to make room for high-rises; before that, houses rarely had more than two or three storeys. Typical features were the richly decorated entrances and mashrabiyas, wooden verandahs jutting out over the street.

# THE SACRED TREE AT MATARIYAH

Plate 115

*January 20, 1839*

*On the 20th, a Sunday, Roberts woke early, and with a hired donkey and a young guide went to Matariyah to see the great sycamore under which the Holy Family is said to have rested during its flight from Herod's soldiers. In fact, what is known as the Tree of Mary was planted in 1672 to replace an older one, already the venue of devout pilgrimages in the Middle Ages. The large village of Matariyah, situated seven and a half miles from Cairo, is still famous today for the chapel dedicated to the Virgin Mary. The sacred tree stands right in front of it, in the middle of a garden with a spring that, according to legend, gushed forth at the command of the baby Jesus. This legend is associated with a far older cult; in nearby Heliopolis, at the time of the great sanctuary of Rameses, there was a sacred tree under which Isis was supposed*

*to have suckled the baby Horus. Roberts carved his name on the bark of the ancient tree and cut off a branch to take as a souvenir to Christine. Although it was a Sunday, Roberts made an exception to the custom of not working (which he did not observe very*

*strictly) and drew the ancient sycamore.*

*As a rather strong wind had started to blow and the sky was full of storm clouds, he decided to hurry to the obelisk, which stood alone on the plain nearby, the sole surviving relic of the glorious ancient city of Heliopolis.*

David Roberts R.A.  L. Haghe lith.                          The Holy Tree, Matareeh

# The Obelisk of Sesostris I, at Heliopolis

Plate 116

*January 20, 1839*

*From Matariyah, Roberts went on to Heliopolis, the place where the historian Herodotus was initiated into the mysteries of the Egyptian priesthood. Founded in ancient times with the name of Iunu and soon afterwards becoming the center from which the worship of the god Ra spread, the native city of the sovereigns of the 5th dynasty is often mentioned in the Bible by the name of On. Heliopolis was one of the main cultural and religious cities in the whole of Egypt; there, the falcon-headed sun god, Ra-Harakhti, Atum, and Mnevi, who had the features of a bull, were worshipped with great devotion. A huge temple, which by the time of Rameses had become the second most important after the one in Thebes, was consecrated to this triad. Its priests were famous throughout the ancient world for their wisdom, and legend has it that even Plato went there to learn from them. Nothing remains of the great sanctuary, built by Amenemhat I on the foundations of an older building, apart from one of the two obelisks that his son and successor, Sesostris I, placed in front of the pylon. The monolith, made of red Aswan granite, is 68 feet tall, and bears the same inscription on all four sides, stating that the sovereign built it to celebrate his first Jubilee. As Heliopolis was near Cairo, the ruins were probably used as*

*a source of building materials over the centuries, which would explain the absence of other monumental remains on the site. As the weather was rapidly deteriorating, Roberts hurriedly sketched the obelisk and mounted his donkey again. Shortly afterwards a violent storm broke, and poor Roberts was soaking wet by the time he reached Cairo.*

**From David Roberts's journal:**

*January 20 - On the way back I was caught in a downpour of exceptional violence, and got so cold that my teeth did not stop chattering for quite a while after I returned home. At the thought of how cold I was, I sincerely feel sorry for all those poor people I have seen clothed only in light cotton garments.*

Obelisk of Heliopolis. 1839

The Nilometer, Island of Rhoda

# THE NILOMETER
## ON THE ISLE OF RHODA

Plate 117

*January 21–22, 1839*

Although he was engrossed in his drawing, Roberts did not neglect the complex organization required for his imminent journey to the Holy Land. A few days earlier he had reached an agreement with the vice-consul, Mr. Walne, for the supply of four camels with which he intended to travel to Syria, and on the morning of the 21st, after packing up the works he had completed so far, he awaited their arrival to conclude the deal. However, the vice-consul brought bad news, all the more shocking because it was totally unexpected; rumor had it that plague had been raging in Jerusalem for three months. A cordon sanitaire had been erected around the city, which meant that if Roberts tried to enter it, he would be placed in quarantine. As he admitted in his journal, "A journey to the Holy Land without seeing Jerusalem would be like visiting England without seeing London." This bad news upset him, but Colonel Campbell suggested that he should make no decision at least until the 24th, when he expected to receive reliable information as to how serious the situation really was. While he waited, Roberts recommenced his explorations, and the next day he returned to the Isle of Rhoda to draw the Nilometer. The adventure proved riskier than expected, as the structure had been converted into a powder magazine, and access was prohibited to all except the guards. Despite the risk of stopping a bullet or having a bad fall, Roberts was determined to complete the task he had set himself. He therefore scaled the outer wall of the structure and from the top hurriedly sketched a study of it, which he completed when he was safe and sound again. Erected circa 715 by the Omayyid Caliphs, who had come from Arabia as conquerors during the 7th century, the Nilometer was similar in concept to those built all over Egypt by the pharaohs, and performed the same task of measuring the level of the river so that the amount of the taxes could be adjusted accordingly. The structure that now survives was built in 861 by Abbasid Caliph al-Mutawakkil. This Nilometer, which is quite sophisticated in design, works on the principle of communicating vessels; the graduated central column is surmounted by a Corinthian capital, and the Kufic inscriptions on the walls are the oldest known in Egypt. The wooden dome was added during a modern restoration.

# THE ANCIENT AQUEDUCT ON THE RIGHT BANK OF THE NILE

Plate 118

*January 22, 1839*

*R*ight opposite the Isle of Rhoda, on the right bank of the Nile, stand the ruins of an ancient aqueduct with the characteristic pointed arches, whose use in the Islamic world preceded Gothic architecture by four centuries; it was 3 miles long, and conveyed water from the Nile to the Citadel. Its route can still be distinguished for a long stretch in the southern districts of the city.

Until the 19th century a canal called the Khalij, which ran alongside the medieval city, conveying water from the Nile to irrigate the fields to the west of Cairo, existed near the massive structure drawn by Roberts, which contained the pumping station of the plant.

The canal, which in 1899 was filled in to become one of the main roads of the metropolis, Sharia Port Said, came into operation when the level of the Nile rose after the summer flood; during the warmest months countless dahabiehs (luxury yachts that once concealed the clandestine vices of the wealthy Cairo bourgeoisie) sailed on the canal. During the rest of the year the entrance to the canal was closed by an earth dike so that its bed could be maintained; the opening day was marked by the most important civil celebration in Cairo, Fath al-Kahlij (the Canal Opening Festival). The pasha himself presided over the ceremony, and the celebrations continued for several days, with music and dancing galore.

# THE TOMBS OF THE CALIPHS AND THE MAUSOLEUM OF EMIR QURQUMAS

<u>Plate 119</u>

*January 23–25, 1839*

While waiting for better news, or at least to dispel the tension created by the consul's visit, which was becoming more agonizing with every day that passed, Roberts visited friends and dined "Turkish-style" with them. In the meantime John Pell tried to persuade Roberts to go with him to Petra, the fabulous Nabataean capital, before continuing to Palestine and Jerusalem. Roberts was very hesitant, however, because he was afraid that this diversion would take too long and would also represent a financial problem for him. In a shrewd move, Pell took the artist to see Linant de Bellefonds, who had painted a series of excellent watercolors of Petra some ten years earlier. Roberts was so struck by them that his resolve wavered considerably.

On January 25 Pell and de Bellefonds accompanied Roberts on yet another excursion to the Tombs of the Caliphs, where the artist sketched what was to be the last of his drawings devoted to the monuments of Cairo. The lithograph portrays a view of the scenic funerary complex built by Emir Qurqumas between 1506 and 1507. The arrangement and appearance of the buildings are very similar to those of the monumental complex erected by Sultan Qaytbay 25 years earlier, and almost seem to be a faithful copy of the same design. Here again, the minaret stands on the right-hand side of the stalactite-work portal, and the sabil-kuttab is built on the left. The quality of the decorations is far inferior, however, and this is particularly evident in the dome over the mausoleum, the outer surface of which is covered with a simple zigzag pattern on a diamond base instead of delicate lacework.

Tombs of the Caliphs, Cairo

David Roberts, R.A.
L. Haghe, lith.

Mosque of Ayed B.

**From David Roberts's journal:**

*January 25 - After the Tombs of the Caliphs, we visited a convent of Dervishes, and went over to the establishment. The cells, which are numerous, seem so small that I should not think it possible for men to lie in them. A small mosque contains the tomb of the saint, covered with a tattered awning. In the evening I drank tea at Mr. Pell's and made two drawings of Egyptian ladies.*

# A GROUP OF DANCING GIRLS

Plate 120

*January 26–February 6, 1839*

On January 26 no news had yet arrived about the situation in Jerusalem; Roberts was increasingly undecided about what to do, and became more and more restless every day. That evening he was invited to dinner by John Pell, and the evening was enlivened by a generous supply of champagne and a performance by pretty dancing girls wearing revealing dresses.

Always susceptible to female charms, Roberts did not hesitate to immortalize the scene, and the fact that this picture concludes our journey to Egypt makes the author seem less austere than Victorian morality and his puritanical daughter might have wished. The days were becoming increasingly tedious, despite the fine weather, when at last the news came, on the morning of the 28th, that the situation in Jerusalem was rapidly improving, and the cordon sanitaire had been lifted.

As the financial problems he was worried about had also been solved by a generous loan of forty pounds from the vice-consul in Alexandria, Robert Thornburn, Roberts finally agreed to accompany Pell as far as Petra. John Kinnear, the son of an Edinburgh banker, also joined the expedition; he formed a deep and lasting friendship with the artist, and dedicated to Roberts a slim volume of travel memoirs published in 1840. The route to Syria took in Mount Sinai, Petra and,

of course, Jerusalem. Pell promised to be ready in a week, and Roberts, having made arrangements for his departure with the diligent Ismail, decided to spend the time left checking over his equipment and painting in oils a view of the city that he intended to give to a friend on his return home.

On January 29 Colonel Campbell provided him with two letters of introduction to the consuls in Jerusalem and Damascus, and a safe-conduct signed by the pasha. On February 6, when the last preparations had been made and Roberts had said good-bye to his friends, he and his new traveling companions set off for Suez, bound for more adventures. But that, as they say, is another story.